The Problem of Hell

D0209742

VILLA JULIE COLLEGE LIBRARY
STEVENSON, MD 21153

THE PROBLEM
OF HELL

Jonathan L. Kvanvig

New York   Oxford
OXFORD UNIVERSITY PRESS
1993

Oxford University Press

Oxford New York Toronto
Delhi Bombay Calcutta Madras Karachi
Kuala Lumpur Singapore Hong Kong Tokyo
Nairobi Dar es Salaam Cape Town
Melbourne Auckland Madrid

and associated companies in
Berlin Ibadan

Copyright © 1993 by Jonathan L. Kvanvig

Published by Oxford University Press, Inc.
200 Madison Avenue, New York, New York 10016

Oxford is a registered trademark of Oxford University Press

All rights reserved. No part of this publication may be reproduced,
stored in a retrieval system, or transmitted, in any form or by any means,
electronic, mechanical, photocopying, recording, or otherwise,
without the prior permission of Oxford University Press.

Library of Congress Cataloging-in-Publication Data
Kvanvig, Jonathan L.
The problem of hell / Jonathan L. Kvanvig.
p. cm. Includes bibliographical references and index.
ISBN 0–19–508487–X
1. Hell—Christianity—Controversial literature. I. Title.
BT836.2.K83 1993 236'.25—dc20   92–44653

2 4 6 8 9 7 5 3 1

Printed in the United States of America
on acid-free paper

75045

Acknowledgments

Many have contributed significantly to this work, and I would like to thank them. In the early stages, discussions with Robert Burch, Daren Cline, Hugh McCann, Robert McKim, and Stacey Pardue were very helpful. When I finished an early draft, Thomas V. Morris was most generous with detailed and well-deserved criticism, and I received helpful comments on later drafts from Glenn Erickson and Michael Hand. In addition, the editorial and production staff at Oxford University Press has been magnificent. The results would have been much less worthwhile without all this help, and for it I am grateful.

Contents

The Problem of Hell

Introduction

One of the most intractable difficulties facing traditional theism is the problem of evil, according to which the belief that God is all-powerful and perfectly good is problematic, given the kinds of evil found in our world. Within those versions of theism of a Judaic heritage—Judaism, Christianity, and Islam—is an especially compelling version of the problem of evil. In addition to the evils that are commonly experienced, in many such traditions a different kind of evil is said to be true of our world. That special kind of evil regards the afterlife, in which some humans are with God forever and some are in hell, which is an excruciatingly bad thing; according to the standard traditions, being in hell is the worst thing that could ever happen to anyone. As with less horrendous evils, the first question is how such an evil is, or could be, justified. The theological portrayals of hell make this question the most difficult for the theist to address. Ordinary pain and evil, it may be thought, can be accounted for if events in the future "make up for" what leads to them, but the evil of hell leads nowhere; at no point in the future will something of value make up for the evil of hell or will some reward be granted to those who endure the suffering of hell. Hell is apparently paradigmatic as an example of truly pointless, gratuitous evil. Thus arises the problem of hell.

This description of the problem of hell and its genesis should make clear that the problem of hell is not limited to any particular religious tradition. As I use the term 'hell', a religious tradition incorporates a doctrine of hell when it affirms an eschatological dimension to reality, that is, when it claims some afterlife conception involving a completion of the point of earthly existence, includes some diagnosis of the ills of the human condition, and offers a course of treatment for these ills. My portrayal of the concept of an afterlife in this work includes any view that maintains that existence continues in some fashion beyond one's earthly death or deaths. These remarks on the scope of my use of the term 'hell' are meant as cautionary, to prevent the misconception that the problem to which this work is devoted is tied in any way to the connotations in contemporary Western culture of the word 'hell', tied as it is to the imaginative language of fire and brimstone and of weeping and gnashing of teeth. Such views fall within the scope of this work, but my investigation is in no way limited to them. Instead, my goal is to treat the problem of hell by paying attention to the philosophical core of such imaginative conceptions, a core that arises in any tradition that claims life beyond death and a future life that can involve the completion, fulfillment, or salvation of a person who will but follow the dictates of a particular religious tradition.

So the problem of hell is a quite general problem for a variety of religious perspectives, and it arises as an instance of the general problem of evil, arguably the worst sort of instance. Moreover, not only is the problem of hell the worst instance of the problem of evil but also there is reason to think the force of this problem for theism is not the same as that of the usual versions of the problem of evil. The following approach to the usual versions of the problem of evil leaves the problem of hell untouched.

The usual versions of the problem of evil come in two varieties, logical and epistemic. A logical version of the problem of evil claims some logical inconsistency between the claim that God is perfectly good and all-powerful and the claim that evil exists. An epistemic version of the problem of evil claims only that the existence of evil provides sufficient reason or evidence to undermine the rationality of believing that a perfectly good and all-powerful God exists. One fruitful approach to the logical problem of evil is Plantingian: Find a sentence that might be true that is obviously compatible with both the omnibenevolence and omnipotence of God and the existence of evil.[1] One such sentence would be 'an omnipotent and perfectly good God created free individuals who make wrong choices, the disvalue of which is overridden by the fact that they are free.' Such a sentence might be true, and it implies both the existence of evil and the existence of an omnibenevolent and omnipotent God.

In the face of this reply, the atheologian has two responses that in the end collapse into one. The first is to abandon the logical problem of evil and focus on the epistemic problem. The other approach is to buttress the claim to logical inconsistency. Instead of claiming that there is an inconsistency between the existence of God, as traditionally conceived, and evil, the atheologian might instead claim that there is an inconsistency between the existence of God and the *kinds of evil* that exist. The atheologian can grant that some kinds of evil—namely, evil that is overridden by some further good—are unproblematic for a traditional conception of God, but not all evils are evidently of this type; some are not obviously overridden by any good.

The theologian can respond to this challenge in one of two ways. The heroic route involves attempting to show that all evils are overridden by some further good. That is, such an approach attempts to say exactly what God has in mind in allowing the evils that exist. Such an approach, I suggest, is not likely to succeed. The other approach is more indirect, attempting to show that this last atheologian response turns the logical problem into an epistemic one. The atheologian claims that not all evil is *evidently* overridden by some further good. Because of the epistemic term used here, this claim is more properly thought of as a version of the epistemic problem of evil. If the epistemic term is dropped, the atheologian is merely claiming that some evils are not overridden by further good, and this claim is not one to which the theologian is committed, nor is it an obvious claim. So, in the face of Plantingian responses to the logical problem of evil, the focus of the debate must turn to the epistemic sphere.

In the epistemic realm, the claim is that the existence of evil provides evidence that there is no God. I suggest that we can best understand the form such an argument takes by considering the claim that some evil appears pointless.[2] If the argument centers on the claim that some evil is in fact pointless, no progress can be made, for the atheologian will claim that some evil is pointless and the theologian will deny this claim. The strategy of the atheologian, however, is to begin with the more circumspect claim that some evil appears to have no point, and here there is some possibility of agreement with the theologian. From this starting point, the atheologian attempts to conclude that it is reasonable to think that God, as traditionally conceived, does not exist. The argument, of course, needs a connecting premise, but the following principle comes to mind to any who are familiar with the epistemological literature of the last few decades: If it appears to person S that sentence p is true, and S has no grounds for doubting the accuracy of this appearance, then it is reasonable for S to believe that p is true. Employing this principle and the circumspect starting point noted previously, the atheologian might seem to have an argument for the disputed claim that some evil is in fact pointless. In the absence of the capacity to say what the point of every evil is, the theologian ought to admit that there are no grounds for doubting the accuracy of any appearance that some evil is pointless.[3] The argument does not demonstrate conclusively that some evil is pointless, but, if it is a good argument, it shows that a reasonable person can believe that some evil is pointless. This latter claim is all the atheologian needs, for if it is reasonable to believe that some evil is pointless, then it is reasonable to believe that there is some evil that God does not care enough to prevent or is not able to prevent. In either case, the traditional conception of God ought to be abandoned.

This epistemic version of the problem of evil can be answered if we pay close attention to the appearance statement involved in the argument. The theologian should distinguish between two claims:

> (A1) It appears to S that *not-p*, where p = *Every evil has a point*; i.e., it appears to S that some evil is pointless,

and

> (A2) It does not appear to S that p, where p = *Every evil has a point.*

The theologian should readily grant the truth of (A2), in the face of the difficulty of saying what the point of every evil is. However, the theologian should not grant the truth of (A1); instead, the theologian should insist that some argument be given for the truth of (A1) by the atheologian.

The distinction between (A1) and (A2) is crucial to the epistemic version of the problem of evil, for the epistemic principle cited previously—if it appears, without grounds for doubt, that p, then it is reasonable to believe that p—requires the truth of (A1) rather than merely (A2). Furthermore, substituting for the epistemic principle in question a different principle that would allow (A2) in place of (A1) results in a false epistemic principle. The new principle would read, "If it does not appear to you that p, and you have no grounds for doubting the accuracy of your perceptual state, then it is reasonable for you to believe *not-p.*" Such a principle underlies arguments from ignorance. To me it does not appear that there is life elsewhere in the universe, and I have no reason to doubt the adequacy of my perceptions here (I have no reason to think I am suffering from a delusion, self-deception, or the like in this matter), but that does not make it reasonable for me to believe that there is no life elsewhere in the universe.

I want to pursue the nature of arguments from ignorance, but first I want to argue that nothing short of this principle will result in a successful attack on theism. In particular, one might try to avoid either (A1) or (A2) by insisting that, on methodological grounds, the theist shoulders some burden of proof that requires having good reason for thinking that every evil has a point. Of course, theists might claim that they do have such a reason, for they have reason to think God exists. But the challenge is meant to be deeper than this response allows, for the challenge attempts to maintain that one needs a reason for thinking that every evil has a point in order for belief in the existence of God to be rational. On such a view, no appeal to the principle that underlies arguments from ignorance is made. In fact, on this challenge, it makes no difference whether either (A1) or (A2) is true. Instead, the challenge arises prior to the precise way in which we encounter the apparent pointlessness of evil, for it maintains that, on methodological grounds alone, theism must find a point for every evil.

The argument is unsuccessful, however, for it insists on a pattern of inference that the theist need not grant. The normal pattern of inference for theists is not from the claim that every evil has a point to the claim that God exists, but rather the opposite. The existence of God, as traditionally conceived, entails, we can grant, that every evil has a point. So the theist can infer that every evil has a point in the same way ordinary folk reject the Cartesian demon hypothesis. In the case of Descartes's evil demon, the usual grounds for inferring that such a hypothesis is false are from the fact that it is obvious that ordinary plants, animals, and other people exist. One does not have to show first that it is reasonable to believe that no Cartesian demon exists in order for the more ordinary claims to be reasonable; the order of inquiry can be, and ordinarily is, opposite while still being fully rational.

So we are left with the version of the epistemic argument from evil that appeals to an epistemic principle underlying arguments from ignorance. I want to explore such arguments further to convey exactly what goes wrong with such arguments and how this failure infects epistemic versions of the problem of evil. First, note that many good arguments bear a superficial resemblance to arguments from ignorance. For example, if I want to know if my children are home, I go into the house and look for them. When I do not see them, I conclude they are not there. At first glance, the argument underlying this inference looks like the argument from ignorance made for the conclusion that there is no life elsewhere in the universe. But there is a crucial and subtle difference between the two, a difference concerning what reasonable attitudes we take toward our perceptual capacities. In the case of knowing that my children are not home, the reasonable attitude is that my perceptual equipment is such, and the environment in which it is operating is such, that if my children were home, they would appear to me to be home, given the actions I have taken. In the case of life elsewhere in the universe, this attitude is not reasonable. That is, it is not (yet) reasonable to think that if there were life elsewhere in the universe, it would appear to us that there is, given our perceptual equipment and the actions we have taken.

So the crucial issue for the epistemic problem of evil concerns the following counterfactual: If every evil had a point, then each evil would appear to us to have a point, given our cognitive capacities and the actions we have taken. I submit that it is not reasonable to believe this claim or to believe that there are any actions we might take that, given our cognitive capacities, would reveal to us the point of every evil, assuming there is one. I submit that believing such claims is no more reasonable than believing the analogous claim about the fundamental physical structure of the universe. We *might* be successful in finding out the ultimate physical structure of the universe; then again, we *might not*. The proper interpretation of these "mights" is denial of the relevant counterfactuals: To say we might and we might not be successful is to say that it is false that we would be successful and false that we would not be successful. This attitude toward our ability to find out the physical structure of the universe is proper because it is reasonable to think that the physical structure of the universe is very difficult for us to ascertain if it can be ascertained at all. The difficulty is apparent from the amount of time and effort that has been expended in the task, with no definitive answers yet found. The same attitude is proper regarding moral matters. The difficulty in the moral realm is apparent from the amount of time and effort expended in the task of developing a full and comprehensive moral theory, with no definitive answers found. I do not say that none of the answers proposed is correct, although I believe that is so; my argument hinges only on the complexity of the task.

In the face of this argument, the crucial premise needed by the atheologian in order to sustain the epistemic argument from evil against the existence of God is the claim that if every evil had a point, thought and effort on our part would reveal to us what that point is. Denying this claim is plausible, but I do not pretend that this discussion settles the issue. My reason for the discussion is to show that a general line can be taken on the problem of evil that fails to address the problem of hell. The problem of hell differs from the general problem of evil in the following way: On the majority of important evils, most theological traditions are silent; they do not say why the evils occur or how such evils fit into the divine scheme. Theologies rarely say why natural disasters occur or what purpose they serve, for example. Such is not the case, however, with the doctrine of hell. The point of hell is fully explicit in the theological traditions in question, and the explicitness of this point gives rise to the problem of hell. Whereas with most evils, the appropriate theological response I favor merely points out that the human condition is one of limited understanding, such a response is of no use when we are told the point of a particular evil. There is no issue regarding hell as to whether it has a legitimate point; the theological traditions that include such a doctrine explicitly state what the point is. Moreover, the problem of hell arises precisely because the point of hell brings about evil that seems in no way capable of being redressed by further good, at any rate, not by *future* good. So even if the general approach I have outlined to the problem of evil is successful, that approach is incapable of providing a solution to the problem of hell, which does not hinge on what we do not understand.

Thus, the problem of hell is severe to the point that a solution to the general problem of evil may provide no help at all in solving the problem of hell. Yet, if the problem of hell is ignored or fails to be solved in some other way, religious traditions that include such a doctrine face a serious dilemma. One of the most forceful presentations of the problem of hell and the reasons for abandoning the doctrine is given by the British metaphysician John McTaggart. He argued[4] that if there is a hell, we could have no good reason to believe it. He reasoned that there is no good empirical evidence to believe in hell, so that if there is a good reason to believe in it, revelation must provide it. Yet, McTaggart continued, the infliction of hell is very wicked, and anyone who would send someone to hell must be vile indeed. In such a case, we could have no good reason to trust such an individual concerning anything of importance to our well-being, for as anyone familiar with the games played by school-yard bullies knows, there is no telling why a vile person would say that something is good or bad for us. The reason may be amusement, to see someone suffer, or for any of a host of other reasons that are compatible with the falsity of what is being said. So if anyone, including God, tells us that there is a hell to shun, McTaggart claims that we could have no good reason to believe that such an individual is telling us the truth. To put the point succinctly, what such a person says undercuts the reliability of the testimony.

We can put this argument in the form of a dilemma that, in honor of its source, I will call "McTaggart's Dilemma." Either there is good reason to believe in hell or there is not. If there is no good reason for belief in hell, no one should believe in it. After all, without some good reason to believe in hell, the option of believing in hell is no better than any other merely possible catastrophe (such as accepting the view that committing suicide immediately is the only way to escape an eternal medieval torture chamber). The point is that there are too many mere possibilities that our lives end in ruin and too many merely possible routes to avoid these possibilities to base any belief on such a mere possibility. So, for the doctrine of hell to be respectable, there must be good reason to believe in it. The difficulty for this option, however, is that the only possible kinds of reasons are self-defeating. The only evidence there might be for hell is based on revelation from the one who can consign us to hell, and yet no one who claims that hell exists and outlines conditions for avoiding hell can be trusted. So, on either horn of the dilemma, the conclusion to be drawn, according to McTaggart, is that belief in hell is not intellectually respectable.

The point of this work is to investigate the problem of hell in order to determine whether a solution to the problem of hell can be provided. In spite of the generality of this problem for a variety of religious perspectives and traditions, I investigate the problem of hell primarily from the standpoint of Christianity and return to a more general perspective only in the last chapter. Such an approach, although perhaps provincial in one sense, will prove beneficial for several reasons. First, the rich variety of alternatives regarding the nature of hell, within the Christian religion does considerable justice to the possibilities any theistic tradition might have in dealing with the problem of hell. Furthermore, the provinciality of approaching the problem from the perspective of one religion is a benefit rather than a cost because, within Christianity, an ongoing dialogue exists between adherents of different positions on the various aspects of an acceptable theology. This intratraditional dialogue has no intertraditional analogue within theistic traditions in general, and any investigation of a theological problem is well served by building on a history of discussion of the problem. Moreover, the worry that provinciality may have its price can be dispelled. Focusing on only one particular tradition would be troublesome if the problem of hell were addressed by paying attention to the connotations that the word 'hell' has in that particular tradition, but this study is not interested in such connotations, except when they shed light on the underlying philosophical account of hell within that tradition. Instead of focusing on imaginative details concerning hell (such as whether it involves fire, gnashing of teeth, and the like), the focus here is on the more abstract theoretical structure any imaginative presentation of the doctrine of hell presupposes. As we shall see, the history of discussion of the problem of hell within Christianity does considerable justice to the variety of abstract theoretical structures to which any approach to the problem of hell might appeal. So the approach to the problem of hell undertaken here from the perspective of Christianity will only benefit from our focused attention and suffer no loss of generality because of it. The results achieved here are easily generalizable to other theistic traditions as well, and in the final chapter I show that our results are generalizable to a more global perspective on the problem of hell.

So, where does the doctrine of hell fit into the scheme of things, according to Christianity? The story of Christianity is portrayed by its adherents as good news. It is the *gospel* of Jesus the Christ. It is good news because, as one follower puts it, God was in Christ reconciling the world to himself. Good news is only one side of the story, however, for Christians have proclaimed not only the benefits brought by the person and work of Jesus the Christ but also the immense costs of failing to declare allegiance to this message. Just as a compliment can also be a threat (think, for example, of a husband, already under investigation for violence due to jealousy, who says to his wife, "You were so beautiful tonight, every guy in the room wanted to dance with you"), the benefits of Christianity are, from a different perspective, the immense costs of hell. Christianity paints a picture of life that enchants many with the splendor of heaven but revolts some of the same and many others with what is at best the squalor of hell and at worst horror beyond description.

The doctrine of hell is no mere addendum to the primary claims of the Christian faith. Instead, the sacred scriptures of the Christian faith found the doctrine in the eschatological nature of Christianity. In this view, the history of the universe is not a pointless wandering in the wilderness of time, but a history with direction to it. Specifically, Christian scriptures maintain that the goal of history is a final consummation of all things in Christ. This consummation, how-

ever, involves a judgment, and a final one at that. It separates once
and for all the sheep and the goats, the first receiving eternal life and
the second going away into eternal punishment.

So at first glance the doctrine of hell is central in the Christian
understanding of the universe and the place of human beings in it.
Yet, the doctrine is controversial, both to those who claim to be
Christians and to those who do not. First, Christians who agree that
there is a heaven to gain and a hell to shun disagree about what hell
is like. Moreover, some who are willing to accept many of the claims
of Christianity are not willing to accept what they perceive to be the
biblical doctrine of hell; they prefer a version of Christianity lacking
this doctrine (if there is such a version). It is also controversial because the purportedly biblical doctrine of hell presents, to many, the
most intractable version of the problem of evil, as we have seen.
Ordinary pain and evil, it may be thought, can in principle be accounted for if events in the future make up for the pain that leads to
them. But the evil of hell leads nowhere; at no point in the future
will something of value make up for the evil of hell or will some
reward be granted to those who endure the suffering of hell. To
many—even to many who would declare their allegiance to the revelation of God in Christ—hell is the paradigm of truly pointless,
gratuitous suffering.

In the face of these controversies, capitulation might seem attractive; that is, the most defensible versions of Christianity jettison
the biblical doctrine of hell. Although some Christians view this
strategy as fawning at the altar of popular opinion, a growing number
favor abandoning the doctrine both within and without Christendom. For example, consider E. S. Chesen's attitude toward hell:
"The concept of hell is also useless and harmful. I suspect that those
evangelists who continue to peddle this asinine idea are beyond
redemption. Inculcation with such a negative entity as hell makes
for intriguing books and horror movies, but does little to promote a
healthy attitude toward religion."[5] Here is expressed a deeply felt
and widespread contemporary attitude toward the topic of this
work: Thinking about hell may be useful if one's imagination tends
toward the horrific, but for more serious interests (such as truth or
the well-being of humanity) religion would be much better off ignoring the topic.

Not only are there popular sentiments such as Chesen's to the
effect that the doctrine of hell is bad for our health, but also there are
theoretical arguments against the doctrine, one of the most interest-
ing being McTaggart's Dilemma, with its recommendation that any

decent religion should abandon the doctrine of hell. These recommendations tell the story of Protestantism in America in the last two centuries. Even the popular press has taken notice of the phenomenon:

> Meantime, observes church historian Martin Marty, "Hell disappeared. And no one noticed." For liberal protestants, hell began to fade in the 19th century along with Calvinism's stern and predestining God. In once Puritan New England, the Universalists decided that God is much too good to condemn anyone to hell, while the Unitarians concluded that humanity is much too good for God to punish—if, indeed, there is a God. Today, hell is theology's H-word, a subject too trite for serious scholarship. When he prepared a Harvard lecture on the disappearance of hell, Marty consulted the indices of several scholarly journals, including one dating back to 1889, and failed to find a single entry.[6]

There is even evidence that the doctrine of hell is losing its force in the last remnants of conservative Protestantism:

> But now, says University of Virginia sociologist James Hunter, author of two books on contemporary evangelicalism, "many evangelicals have a difficult time conceiving of people, especially virtuous nonbelievers, going to hell." In one of his studies, for example, Hunter asked evangelical students if they thought Gandhi was in hell. "They recognized that by their own theology Gandhi should be in hell, but the idea made them extremely nervous. . . ." He concludes that evangelicals are tempering their images of hell: "People say now, 'I think there is a hell but I hope it will be a soul-sleep.'"[7]

The lesson here is clear: The theological trend of the last few centuries strays dramatically from a central feature of historical Christianity. Even those whose theological outlooks require the doctrine find it disquieting, and alternative outlooks not requiring the doctrine find ready acceptance among a population whose conception of God leaves little room for the language of fire and brimstone.

The motivation for abandoning hell is easily understood, given the controversial nature of the doctrine and the millstone it can be around the neck of any serious attempt to assuage intellectual concerns over the truth of Christianity. Regardless of the attractiveness of abjuration, however, this approach is not promising. Innovation in matters religious has its price. For one thing, originality has usually been seen as a vice rather than a virtue in the theological traditions in question, and whether abandoning the doctrine of hell would amount to merely altering the tradition or forsaking it altogether, is far from clear. For another, when religious traditions become too malleable, the labels attached to them—'Christianity', 'Islam', 'Judaism'—come to be more akin to the labels for political parties; where the goal is often only to preserve the title, without much substantive intellectual commitment attached to what is labeled. Developments of this sort within a tradition, religious or not, are often best seen as degenerative in that they signal a way of conceptualizing the theoretical landscape that is not very useful. Just as a classification of animals into terrestrial, aquatic, and aerial gives way to the more fecund biological classification schemes that put some of each of these categories in the same group, theological innovation may result in a situation where the terms for various traditions do not classify in a way that provides the deepest and most useful understanding of the variety of options a person can take toward matters of spirituality. Yet, if anything is central to a religious perspective, it is that the core of that perspective is crucial to a proper conception of spirituality; that is, any proper way of conceiving of the theoretical alternatives must include it as one of the fundamental alternatives.

More important, abandonment of the doctrine is not promising because some such doctrine is central to the point of the major theistic traditions. In this instance, it is central to Christianity that the person and work of Jesus have a point; humanity is in need of something that Christians maintain God has provided in Christ. The traditional conception of hell that has been deemed problematic—and correctly so, as we shall see—is but one way of preserving these central points of Christianity, and we fail to appreciate the problem of hell if we do not first understand the necessity for Christianity to offer some account of the destiny of humanity apart from salvation through Christ. In sum, a Christian account of hell describes our destiny beyond this life apart from the work of God in Christ, and any approach that makes that work significant beyond the grave cannot help presupposing some account of hell.

Of course, inferring the traditional doctrine of hell from the need for some such account would be an extraordinarily bad argument, for many alternatives have been and might be proposed. One such option dismisses any notion of an afterlife altogether. Perhaps our destiny apart from Christ is an earthly life missing an important dimension. Perhaps, for example, the story of Christ and the intrusion of the divine into human history is a mythical call on behalf of the liberation of the human spirit from capitalist, racist, or sexist oppression. More metaphysically, perhaps the point of the story of

Jesus is to be explained in terms of the eternal incarnation of the divine Idea in the human species as a whole and in its historically developing general consciousness, or perhaps the story points to the possibility of this incarnation and the call to all of us to aid in the realization of this possibility.[8] Whatever the details of the alternative, however, the outline is the same. Even if all there is to life is our three score and ten, one might hold—and some do—that such a life lived in response to the call of God in Christ is a life eternal in its character as compared with its alternatives.

For many others, however, such an emaciated eschatology is hardly deserving of the label 'Christian'. First, some of these approaches require such a radical revision of our ordinary metaphysical conception of the importance of the individual and what sorts of things can legitimately count as spiritual entities that they have little persuasive appeal to most. Consider, for example, the Hegelian view that the point of the story of Jesus has to do with the eternal incarnation of the divine Idea in the human species as a whole. What I have written is not an argument against such accounts, of course, but an explanation of why such versions of Christianity are not likely to be serious competitors in the marketplace of ideas; they will not be, as William James puts it, "live options" for most individuals.

Second, those options that sit better with our ordinary metaphysical conception of the universe still tend to be unsatisfying when they limit their eschatology to this life. Two lines of thought lead to this conclusion. The first is moral in character, and the second has to do with the nature of God's love. Regarding the first point, most of us feel deeply that wrongdoing should be rectified in some way and that those who have suffered need to be recompensed. Even if, as Christians maintain, God's goodness causes him to wait patiently in the hope that forgiveness and reconciliation can fulfill the demands of justice, there is still a story to be told of what justice demands, should such reconciliation fail. The other side of this coin concerns the large percentage of the world's population who are harried and hapless. For Christianity to forget in its eschatology the plight of the majority of the world's population and the demands of fairness that their suffering be redressed would be gross cultural bigotry. These insights form a core component of an adequate Christian understanding of the human condition, and in historical Christianity these insights have been given a distinctly eschatological flavor: God's purposes in allowing the wrongdoing, pain, and suffering of this vale must at some point have been achieved, and at that point, at the end of "this age," recompense is due. Any version of Christianity limited in significance to the present earthly life fails to address the demands of our sense of justice and fairness, for obviously, evildoers sometimes evade punishment in this life and those who suffer often do not deserve it.

Of course, that much of the pain and suffering in the world goes unrequited may be just a regrettable fact about life. My point is not so much to argue that, if there is a God, he ultimately must balance the scales of justice, but rather to explain why many individuals attracted to Christianity are attracted only to a version with significance beyond the grave. That is, I make no claims here regarding the truth of the sentiments that give rise to allegiance to Christianity in traditional garb, but instead seek only to make understandable the attractiveness of versions of Christianity requiring a doctrine of hell.

As noted previously, the second reason some find attractive only a version of Christianity with postmortem significance concerns the Christian view of God as a loving God. The work of God in Christ is rooted, Christianity claims, in his love for human beings; and as Aquinas claimed, love involves not only willing good for the one loved but also desire for union with the beloved. Whatever the blessings of the Christian life, the earthly experience of the believer rarely if ever conveys a sense of complete union with the divine. What Christians believe *will be* is still *not-yet*, even at the moment of death. Even those moments of highest fulfillment in the Christian experience of God often do not satisfy completely, and even if they do, those moments are still just moments. They pass away into the reality of other moments in which the character of one's experience is that of absence, that of something missing; and even when one is not immediately aware of this quality, it is nonetheless there to be discovered by the simplest reflection. So any account of Christianity that addresses the deepest longings of the human breast has to posit an afterlife in which we no longer see, as St. Paul put it, "through a glass darkly, but face to face."

Against the backdrop of these hopes, desires, and longings the Christian doctrine of the incarnation is set in relief. The consensus among Christians throughout history has been that the deepest desires and longings of the human heart have been addressed by the creator of the universe in Jesus the Christ. The significance of the work of God in Christ is not limited to our earthly existence, but encompasses all eternity, for only such an action befits the incomprehensible love of God and only such an initiative on the part of the divine could meet the longings present in the soul of humanity. Even in this incomplete skeletal outline of some of the features of histori-cal Christianity, however, the problem of hell emerges. Even if God's redemptive purposes extend to all humankind and even if his purposes were sure to be achieved, Christianity still must include an account of *what would have happened to humanity* apart from God's intervention in Christ if Christianity is to explain adequately the point of that intervention. Any such account of what would have happened had God not intervened in Christ involves the topic of hell in some way, even if the view of hell that results is far from tradi-tional.

In this regard one other point is worth making. In an age of compromise between various religious traditions, some find attrac-tive a merging of Eastern thought with Christian thought. One such eclectic approach introduces the cycle of rebirth into Christianity by maintaining that those not yet fit for heaven are reincarnated again into the earthly realm to try again. This approach fails to introduce anything new of philosophical substance pertaining to the problem of hell. On this supposedly synergistic approach, two options are open regarding the doctrine of hell. In the first, hell is identified with the cycle of rebirth, in that human destiny beyond this present earthly life apart from the work of God in Christ is to be trapped in this cycle. This account of hell is quite unorthodox, and we shall investigate it in Chapter 2. The present point is just that this view does not circumvent the problem of hell; instead, it only offers an unorthodox account of hell. In the second option, the cycle of rebirth is a precursor to the final alternatives of heaven and hell. This view holds that the cycle of rebirth provides for numerous second chances at redemption. Such a view does not escape the problem of hell, however, for it must say what would happen if an individual were to reject the entire multitude of chances comprised by the cycle of rebirth. This account does not escape the problem of hell either, but rather only postpones it. Instead of being confronted with hell after death, one is confronted with it only after the cycle of rebirth is complete (whenever that might be). In any case, the problem of hell cannot be avoided merely by altering or supplementing the tradi-tional Christian conception of the afterlife. Instead, the only way to avoid the problem of hell is to limit the significance of Christianity to earthly life, which is, to many, too high a price to pay for solving the problem of hell.

So, to a very large portion of Christendom, if there is to be a satisfying and complete explanation of what, according to Chris-tianity, God did for humanity in Christ, there is no escape from the problem of hell. I am not arguing, of course, that traditional Christianity is correct and all other conceptions of Christianity are mistaken. My aim at this point, to repeat, is explanatory, not polemical. I have tried to make clear what the idea of abandoning the doctrine of hell comes to, and why compromising with nontraditional conceptions of Christianity by abandoning the doctrine of hell can be undesirable. I have also wanted to make clear that the motivations for such a noncompromising attitude do not arise because such individuals are unduly fastidious; the attitudes, desires, and longings I have cited are common to the human experience. For such individuals, Christianity is attractive only in its traditional garb, with an eschatology positing a point to the life and work of God in Christ that extends beyond the grave. For such individuals, whether the doctrine of hell is given its traditional rendition or some other formulation, no emancipation from that doctrine is possible without abandoning Christianity itself or succumbing to the viewpoint that the deepest longings of their hearts will go unsatisfied.

The course I counsel begins by accepting that there is no satisfactory Christian alternative to the difficult theological and philosophical task of formulating and defending a conception of hell. This book is dedicated to just this task. For those convinced that Christianity needs no such doctrine, take this work solely in terms of the historical point that the doctrine of hell has been a central component in traditional Christianity. My view of the matter, which I have not defended here, is that the doctrine has more than historical significance; but for those of a different persuasion, the historical significance of the doctrine is reason enough to raise the question of whether a philosophically and theologically acceptable formulation of the doctrine can be given, and thus whether a philosophically and theologically defensible version of historical Christianity can be found.

For the most part, the constraints that govern this work are philosophical in character, but a word about the theological constraints is in order. One such constraint undergirds the project: I assume for discussion of the problem of hell that God exists and that existence is not bounded by the grave. In the context of considering the doctrine of hell in historical Christianity, however, another theological issue arises. This book is part of a growing body of literature that investigates the theoretical power of historical Christianity,[9] and the results here and elsewhere show a philosophical richness to this tradition that is masked by a cultural drift away from it. Yet, no focus on the adequacy of historical Christianity can succeed if it ignores the theological constraints arising from the scriptures of the Christian religion. This issue is addressed at the end of chapter 4, where I consider to what extent the philosophical investigation of the problem of hell fit the scriptures of the Christian religion. Because this work aims not only to consider whether there is a solution to the problem of hell but also to be sensitive to the theological and religious contexts in which the doctrine of hell lives, this issue is important. A philosophical solution to the problem of hell that did violence, of necessity, to theological and religious sensibilities would be unfortunate. The section addressing this issue can be seen as a case study of whether the philosophical account can be reconciled with the lived experience of a particular religion. Even if such a reconciliation is possible—and I argue it is—that provides no guarantee that, in any other religious context, such a reconciliation is possible. Investigating the issues further would require more space than we have here, however, and a positive result in the case of Christianity at least provides hope for positive results for other religions as well.

In order to raise this issue in a fashion that is fair to the philosophical analysis that follows, I must caution against identifying the biblical conception of hell with the traditional theology concerning hell. First, I consider the traditional doctrine of hell, perhaps the most common one in the history of Christian thought on hell. In summary form, it maintains that hell is a place where some people are punished eternally with no possibility of escape. We can analyze this doctrine, which I call here the strong view of hell, into four separate components:

> (H1) The Anti-Universalism Thesis: some persons are consigned to hell;
>
> (H2) The Existence Thesis: hell is a place where people exist, if they are consigned there;
>
> (H3) The No Escape Thesis: there is no possibility of leaving hell, and nothing one can do, change, or become in order to get out of hell, once one is consigned there; and
>
> (H4) The Retribution Thesis: The justification for and purpose of hell is retributive in nature, hell being constituted so as to mete out punishment to those whose earthly lives and behavior warrant it.

I begin with this doctrine primarily because the pragmatics of intellectual effort counsel against reinventing the wheel. The strong view of hell is a biblical conception of hell in that this view implies a finality to the separation of those who receive eternal life from those who receive eternal punishment. If we are to be justified in pursuing a theological and philosophical alternative to this view, we need first to find some reason to be dissatisfied with this traditional understanding of hell.

A different reason for starting with the strong view might be that one is convinced that this view of hell is taught in scripture, that it is *the* biblical conception of hell. This reason is not mine; moreover, the strong view is but one of several accounts of hell that are, arguably, compatible with the claims of scripture. Instead of addressing the matter here, I take it up at the end of chapter 4. I mention it here only to avoid the misunderstanding that in criticizing the strong view of hell I am criticizing the only conception of hell compatible with a traditional view of scriptural authority within Christianity. A piece of theology may have many virtues including the virtue of being true, but separating good and adequate theology from that which is explicitly and directly taught in scripture, is crucially important. A theology is, fundamentally, a theory developed by human beings about the divine. Historically, the task of constructing an adequate Christian theology has been the task of accounting for the data of scripture and Christian experience. As with all cases of theory construction, our understanding of the data is sometimes altered by our theoretical investigations, and the case is no different in theology. Often theologies have led to a dismissal of some type of purportedly Christian experience, and, more so in recent centuries than in those more removed in time, the theological task has led many to an altered understanding of which portions of the Bible constitute data for which a theology must account. The important point, though, is not the particular relationship between data and theory or the more critical attitude toward scripture and the data to be elicited from it that contemporary theology takes, but rather that theologies are theories. They are an attempt to explain certain data, and any such accounting results in a theory that goes beyond the data it is constructed to explain. In classic scientific examples, theories go beyond the data they are to explain by positing the existence of unobserved and perhaps unobservable entities, such as atoms, electrons, quarks, and the like. In Christian theology, even for conservative Christians, theological theories go beyond the statements of scripture and the record of Christian experience. Such a theology formulates systematically certain claims not (always) themselves found in scripture but thought to be the best explanation of the insights in scripture and the pith of Christian experience.

It would be surprising if nothing in scripture supported the traditional conception of hell; indeed, as shown in chapter 4 much is to be found on its behalf. Nonetheless, thinking that scripture is compatible only with that view would be a mistake. In any nonconservative view about the authority of scripture, decisions need to be made about what parts of scripture are more theologically significant than others; indeed, even assuming the most conservative Christian position on the authority of scripture, other decisions still would have to be made. These decisions include which passages to treat as primary and which to interpret in light of the primary passages, and which passages to take figuratively and which to take nonfiguratively. Even from the most conservative viewpoint concerning the authority and reliability of the Bible, there can be no immediate and direct scriptural grounds for making such decisions. To attempt to find such a reason is by its very nature circular. Our canons of interpretation are necessarily our own canons, and any attempt to relieve ourselves of the weighty philosophical obligation to develop and defend such canons by appeal to "the text" is obscurantist. Once we recognize the theoretical status of these decisions, seeing that a theology of hell cannot be read off from the scriptural record is no longer difficult.

My point is not that any interpretation of scripture is arbitrary, for what I have claimed is compatible with there being a truth to the matter of what authority scripture should have for the Christian. My point is rather that scripture alone cannot settle these issues. We do great injustice to the discipline of theology if we pretend that it is anything but a fully theoretical enterprise, and we would show disdain for the seriousness of the theoretical task if we were to pretend that appeal to the text can replace hard thinking.

So, I begin with the strong view for pragmatic reasons and not because I think it is the scriptural view of hell. I assume in what follows that the strong view is not explicitly endorsed anywhere in scripture. For those inclined toward conservative positions on the authority of scripture, this fact is serendipitous, for I argue in chapter 1 that the strong view of hell is objectionable. In particular, I argue that it is subject to McTaggart's Dilemma, that the only possible reasons for believing the strong view are undercut by the strong view itself. In spite of its defects, however, the strong view is superior to the standard alternatives to it, a point I argue at length in chapter 2.

This conclusion then points the way toward an account of hell that is theologically and philosophically adequate. The strong view cannot be accepted as it stands, but the ultimate conclusion I wish to draw is that the best piece of theology about hell is much closer to the strong view than to any of its extant competitors.

Regardless of the particular strategy one takes in addressing the problem of hell, I hope I have made clear here why the problem of hell cannot be ignored. Contrary to the claim of an earlier quote, that "hell is theology's H-word, a subject too trite for serious scholarship," there is good reason, even overwhelming reason, for a careful and scholarly consideration of the doctrine of hell, for most theistic traditions imply that existence is not bounded by the grave and thus require such a doctrine. Yet, such a doctrine raises immediately the problem of evil, a version that stands untouched by some perhaps plausible responses to the more general problem of evil. My strategy is to investigate the problem of hell as it arises in Christianity, and the structure of this work is as follows. It begins by eliciting and considering objections, both theological and philosophical, to the strong view of hell. In large part, these objections summarize the critical discussion of the doctrine of hell within Western Christianity in the past centuries. The aim of chapter 1 is to present the variety of complaints against the strong view in a dialectical structure that allows the reader to grasp the significance of a bewilderingly complex history of criticism and response. These objections are severe enough that some changes are required in the doctrine, and the second chapter considers some simple alternatives to the strong view of hell. These alternatives are heterodox in nature and include the standard views of hell that appear more favorable to our contemporary culture: universalism, second chance doctrines, annihilationism, and the like. The discussion shows that these views cannot survive theological and philosophical scrutiny, not even scrutiny that employs no claims peculiar to the Christian community. Thus difficulties plague not only the orthodox view of hell but standard heterodox views as well. This situation calls for a deeper investigation of the need for the doctrine of hell and its place in relation to the Christian account of the nature of God and to the Christian view of the sinfulness of humanity. I undertake this investigation in the final chapters, where I present an account of the nature of hell adequate to the demands of Christianity. I argue that this account is firmly grounded in Christian claims concerning the nature of God (although these claims are not unique to Christianity). It is fully compatible with the biblical portrayal of God as a God of love, and it also remains faithful to the biblical record about the seriousness of sin and the reality of hell. Moreover, I argue that the existence of hell is fully compatible with the perfect goodness of God as well as his unbounded love toward all humanity. In sum, the account here has these virtues precisely because it explains the nature of both heaven and hell in terms of God's love for the entire created order. The conclusion I draw is that the Christian doctrine of hell is subject to no compelling difficulty and thus that the problem of hell is not unresolvable.

Notes

1. Alvin Plantinga has pursued this strategy over several decades. The most developed version appears in *The Nature of Necessity* (Oxford: Clarendon Press, 1974).

2. In what follows, I borrow heavily from a growing literature on the subject. See, e.g., M. B. Ahern, *The Problem of Evil* (London: Routledge & Kegan Paul, 1971); William P. Alston, "The Inductive Argument from Evil and the Human Cognitive Condition," in *Philosophical Perspectives 5: Philosophy of Religion*, James E. Tomberlin, ed. (Atascadero, Calif.: Ridgeview Publishing Co., 1991); F.J. Fitzpatrick, "The Onus of Proof in Arguments about the Problem of Evil," *Religious Studies* 17 (1981): 21–35; Bruce Reichenbach, *Evil and a Good God* (New York: Fordham University Press, 1982); and Stephen Wykstra, "The Humean Obstacle to Evidential Arguments from Suffering: On Avoiding the Evils of 'Appearance'," *International Journal for Philosophy of Religion* 16 (1984):73–93.

3. There are questions surrounding this claim having to do with whether God must create the best. I bypass these questions here, granting the claim in the text, for I believe the problem of evil can be answered even when this claim is granted.

4. In *Some Dogmas of Religion* (London, 1906), section 177.

5. E. S. Chesen, *Religion May Be Hazardous to Your Health* (New York, 1972), p. 93.

6. Kenneth L. Woodward, "Heaven," *Newsweek*, March 29, 1989, p. 54.

7. Ibid.

8. See, for example, the Hegelian-infected concluding apologetic sections of D. F. Strauss's *The Life of Jesus*, first published in 1835.

9. Among these works one should include Richard Swinburne, *The Coherence of Theism* (Oxford, 1977); Alvin Plantinga, *God, Freedom and Evil* (New York, 1974); Thomas V. Morris, *The Logic of God Incarnate* (Ithaca, N.Y., 1986); Thomas V. Morris, ed., *The Concept of God* (New York, 1987) and *Divine and Human Action* (Ithaca, N.Y., 1988); and Thomas P. Flint, ed., *Christian Philosophy* (Notre Dame, 1990).

1

The Strong View of Hell

The view of hell held by traditional Christianity I am calling the strong view of hell. We have seen that this view involves four separable commitments:

> (H1) The Anti-Universalism Thesis: Some persons are consigned to hell;
>
> (H2) The Existence Thesis: Hell is a place where people exist, if they are consigned there;
>
> (H3) The No Escape Thesis: There is no possibility of leaving hell and nothing one can do, change, or become in order to get out of hell, once one is consigned there; and
>
> (H4) The Retribution Thesis: The justification for hell is retributive in nature, hell being constituted to mete out punishment to those whose earthly lives and behavior warrant it.

Before we move into the substance of this chapter, a few words of explanation about the strong view are in order. First, different pictures of hell are compatible with these theses. For example, some hold that the denizens of hell are actively tormented by fire, whereas others consider separation from certain blessings associated with heaven to be punishment enough.[1] In either case, the theory is committed to the list and therefore subscribes to the strong view of hell. Second, although many Christians hold that all persons in hell receive the same punishment, this interpretation is not the only one possible. It is, however, the most demanding version to defend. I begin by considering what I call "the equal punishment version of the strong view," which involves a commitment to (H1)–(H4) in such a way that all persons in hell receive the same punishment. We shall investigate varieties of the strong view that do not maintain equality of punishment in hell after discussing this strong view. The third and final preliminary point about the strong view concerns a trivial way to avoid that view, which I propose to ignore here. Many Christians have maintained the doctrine of the harrowing of hell, according to which Christ, between his death and his resurrection, preached to the inhabitants of hell, securing the release of many through their faith in him and his message.[2] This view involves a denial of the No Escape Thesis, although it is quite weak. Such Christians have also held that the harrowing of hell is a unique and unrepeatable event. (The view that inhabitants of hell can be released at times other than between Christ's death and resurrection is discussed in the next chapter.) Such Christians thus hold to a Modified No Escape Thesis, according to which anyone consigned to hell can *no longer* escape. This way of avoiding the strong view of hell is not significant for our purposes, for there is no practical difference, regardless of which thesis is true. The only time when this way of affirming the Modified No Escape Thesis would have had any practical significance would have been prior to the resurrection. Hence in what follows I ignore this alternative to the strong view.

The strong view of hell, as noted in the Introduction, is no longer a popular view of hell. The point of this chapter is to investigate the charges brought against this view of hell, of which two are the focus of attention here. One comes from within the moral sphere and is often voiced in terms of the view that conservative Christians worship a "vindictive" God. The charge underlying this claim is that there is something morally unacceptable about the strong view of hell. The other charge can be elicited from the sociological or anthropological attitude taken by many toward those who hold the doctrine of hell. Many in our culture view the advocates of hell as curiosity pieces. Those who advocate the doctrine of hell may perhaps stimulate in others the desire to know or understand those with differing cultural practices, but the views themselves hold no attraction. They are museum pieces only.

This indifference to Christians' claims results from two quite different forces. One is the pull of atheism and agnosticism in our culture, for anyone who holds either view will find the doctrine of hell too laden with presuppositions about the existence of God to spark an inclination to believe the doctrine. Because this book's purpose is not to address the epistemological issues surrounding the rationality of theism, I do not devote any further attention to this lack of interest in the doctrine of hell. The other force is felt even by theists and is clearly relevant to the purposes of this work. This doctrine of hell appears to many theists to be completely unrelated to any reasonable understanding of the nature and character of God. The museum piece image of the doctrine is sure to follow this outlook in that the doctrine would at best be only an unrelated addendum to the core of Christian theology.

Whereas the first difficulty is moral, the second is conceptual and epistemological. The first concerns whether consigning anyone to hell is morally acceptable. The second difficulty concerns the motivation and justification for the doctrine of hell, that is, whether consigning anyone to hell is consistent with God's nature and whether there could be a good enough reason to think that God *must* send anyone there. To appreciate the character of the second difficulty more fully, let us suppose for a moment that the moral objection can be answered. If it can, it follows that the strong view of hell is consistent with God's moral character. Even so, God's character has more to it than just the moral part, and to many hell seems incompatible with, in particular, God's loving nature, regardless of whether it is compatible with his moral character. If one is inclined to think about God and hell along these lines, then the strong view of hell has both epistemological and conceptual problems, even if it can escape the moral problem. If the doctrine of hell is inconsistent with God's loving nature, then God could have no good reason to send anyone to hell, and thus those who think God could send someone to hell must have a distorted concept of God—one with insufficient room for divine love.

Pursuing the moral objection to its logical end will reveal the substance and merit of the second objection in an especially revealing way, so we can approach both objections by concentrating on the first.

The Moral Objection to the Equal Punishment Version of the Strong View

The features of this version of the strong view that elicit objection are two: that every individual in hell receives the same punishment and that this punishment is infinite in nature. Addenda to these features of hell in terms of fire, brimstone, torture, and torment may call out additional epithets, such as "barbaric," "perverse," and the like; even apart from these additional features, however, this version of the strong view is thought by many to be objectionable simply because it is *unfair* and *unjust*: unfair, because not everyone is equally guilty; unjust, because not all sin, if any, deserves an infinite punishment.

These objections must be answered. Defenders of the strong view cannot just say, for example, that God makes the rules or that we are in no position to question the divine edicts. About the first response, in some sense God may be the sole author of everything, including morality.[3] No account of God as the author of morality will do, however, if God's choices in this regard are taken to be arbitrary or capricious. For example, any account of God as the author of morality is inadequate that implies that, if God were to command us to torture infants, doing so would be proper. Instead, because God is perfectly good, that God would command such a thing is inconceivable, impossible. When faced with a moral objection to our theology, we cannot say that God makes the rules and that is all there is to it. If the objection is well taken—if, in fact, that aspect of the theology in question is morally objectionable—it is simply impossible that God makes the rules in that way.

Much the same answer should be given to the second response, that we are in no position to question the divine edicts. God is justified in doing, and able to do, as God wills, and we have no right or power to interfere. However, God is perfectly good, and no perfectly good being could do anything that is morally objectionable. So, we cannot grant the soundness of the objection while maintaining that we should not raise such objections, for that position is inconsistent with the perfect goodness of God. Yet, if the objection is unsound, the best response to the objection includes saying what is wrong with it instead of merely pointing out the impropriety of raising it.

In order to explain why the objection is not well taken, defenders of this version of the strong view must cite some moral principle that explains why God justifiably treats persons as their view claims he does. For example, when Truman's decision to drop the atomic bomb on Japan is questioned on moral grounds, the response invokes some moral principle. One response might be that dropping the bomb resulted in fewer deaths (or fewer American deaths) than would have resulted had Japan been invaded. Here the relevant moral principle is that the right thing to do is to prevent as many deaths (or American deaths) as possible, and then the issue turns on the truth or falsity of the cited principle.[4]

If we look at some general features of cases of wrongdoing, we can begin to get an idea of what defenders of the equal punishment version of the strong view might say in defense of it. Two features are obvious in ordinary cases: first, the evil or harm caused or the suffering experienced by another; and, second, the intended harm, whether the intention is ever realized or not. Little reflection is needed to see that these factors do not, by themselves, provide sufficient material for answering the moral objection to the equal punishment version of the strong view. This version claims that all sin deserves the same, infinite punishment, yet some persons cause more actual harm than others,[5] and some intend more harm than others.[6] So, the first two factors do not seem sufficient to justify equality of punishment. Moreover, it is difficult to see how any reasonable accounting of the amount of actual and intended harm could, of necessity, require an infinite punishment. To deserve an infinite punishment on the basis of actual or intended harm would seem to require that every person have caused or willed an infinite amount of harm, and the evidence we have suggests that not all have done that. Yet, the equal punishment version of the strong view of hell claims that just such an infinite punishment is deserved.

The lesson is this: A defense against the moral objection must appeal to some moral feature other than those we have cited thus far. Defenders of this version of the strong view claim just such a feature, namely, the nature of the individual who is the object of (actual or intended) harm. Those of us who are familiar only with democratic social institutions have difficulty appreciating the existence of this feature, but it would have been obvious to members of feudal societies and others involving classes or castes that who we wrong greatly affects the seriousness of the wrong. Such a defense appeals to the "guilt is proportional to the status of the offended party" principle (the "status principle," for short). According to this principle, guilt incurred by wrongdoing is proportional not only to the severity of actual or intended harm but also to the kind of being against whom the act is committed.

Some easily grant such a feature to morality because their moral experiences involve participation in nonegalitarian societies. If the only support for this principle arises from such experiences, however, the principle would hardly be of much use in defending the equal punishment version of the strong view of hell. That these experiences are grounded in the moral dimension of life rather than in the unprincipled and transient character of societal organization is far from obvious. In the end, the principle may have no other support, but this defense of the equal punishment version of the strong view cannot be dismissed on these grounds yet. Defenders of the principle can give examples suggesting that it does not rely solely on the experiences of members of societies with clearly structured classes. One such example is that the moral guilt, if any, incurred by killing a plant is quite different from that incurred by killing a human being. So, perhaps cases of wrongdoing have this additional feature, as defenders of this version of the strong view maintain, and perhaps this additional feature might be useful in defending this version against the moral objection to it.

Consider, then, how the status principle might be used in response to this objection. According to the status principle, what punishment a person deserves is determined by the amount of guilt accruing to that person, but how much guilt accrues to a person is not simply a matter of how much harm has been done or intended. Rather, even the smallest amount of harm might deserve an infinite punishment. How could this be? According to the status principle, the punishment deserved is determined by two factors; the status of the being affected and the amount of actual or intended harm involved. We can think of this principle, then, in terms of a mathematical function. A mathematical function operates on its arguments and generates an output. For example, addition operates on two numbers and generates their sum as output. Just so, the amount of punishment deserved is generated by determining what function on harm and status is appropriate. In particular, given the right function, an infinite punishment might be deserved and this principle thereby employed to justify the strong view of hell.

One question about this defense is whether the right function is one that can carry the weight required by the equal punishment version of the strong view. The answer is not immediately obvious, and so some investigation is called for into what we might call the function aspect of the status principle. In addition, we need to consider how the status of an individual is measured. Use of the status principle in defending the equal punishment version of the strong view of hell clearly relies on wrongs done against God, which would seem to be the best chance this version has of finding the right combination of status, function on status, and harm to warrant an infinite punishment. Yet if this defense is to succeed, it needs some account of how status is determined that yields a true interpretation of the status principle. For example, God would have the highest possible status if status were measured in terms of longevity. Using this measure, the longer an individual has existed, the worse the harming that individual would be. Yet, if the "guilt proportional to the status of the offended party" principle is interpreted using this account of status, it is surely false; murdering an infant is surely no less wrong than murdering an adult (all else being equal). Hence, the plausibility of using this principle in defense of the equal punishment version of the strong view of hell requires some account of how status is determined.

One final aspect remains to this defense of this version of the strong view against the moral objection. As already noted, that God is brought into the picture as the one against whom wrong is intended is crucial for this defense. Otherwise, the seriousness of our wrongs would vary from one person to another, as would deserved punishments. Moreover, without bringing God into the picture, perhaps no wrongs, and at most only a very few wrongs, done against other individuals could be serious enough to warrant infinite punishment. Therefore, use of this principle relies centrally on bringing God into the picture. According to this defense, all deserve hell because all have sinned *against God*.

Which sin or how much sin must a person commit against God to justify infinite punishment?[7] There is a plausible argument that one sin alone done against God must be enough if the equal punishment version of the strong view is to be defended. Defenders of this version maintain that what we do in our earthly lives determines our destiny in the afterlife, so the justification for an infinite punishment must be found among the finite number of wrongs we commit during our finite earthly existence. If one sin alone is not enough to warrant infinite punishment, no function on number of sins will do either, for any such function would be completely arbitrary in drawing the line where it did. For example, suppose the claim is that sixteen sins are not enough to warrant an infinite punishment, but seventeen are. The natural response is to wonder why that would be so. We would be at a loss to find any principled reason for drawing the line at a particular number of sins.[8]

Yet, if one sin against God is enough, which sin might it be? There are constraints on what a defender of the equal punishment version of the strong view might claim here, for such a defender is already committed to the view that any sinner is headed for hell apart from the redemptive work of Christ. This commitment leaves the defender of this version of the strong view with two options. The first is to find some particular sin against God that is claimed to deserve an infinite punishment and that no (nondivine) human avoids committing. The difficulty with this option is thinking of an act that would satisfy that description. The difficulties with this approach incline defenders of the equal punishment version of the strong view to the second option, which is to claim that any sin whatsoever done against God is of sufficient disvalue to justify an infinite punishment. There are no distinguished sins, the defender of this version of the strong view might claim, for all sin is of equal disvalue when committed against God.

In order, then, for this version of the strong view to be defensible, offenses against God must all have the same ultimate moral status. Yet with this claim alone the defense cannot rest. In addition, it must establish that every person sins against God at some time or other. If a person avoids sinning against God, the equal punishment version of the strong view of hell would still be objectionable because it implies that all people are headed for hell apart from God's intervention on their behalf.

So the question now is, When does a person sin against God? The two views one might hold here are a restrictive view and a perfectly general view. In the perfectly general view, every sin is a sin against God. In the restrictive view, only some sins are sins against God. If only some particular sins are against God, presumably they would be those in which God is the intentional object of some action. For example, if I throw a rock and to hit my cat with it, then the cat is the intentional object of this action. Just so, the restrictive view about sinning against God would seem likely to claim that one sins against God when and only when one "aims at" or "strikes at" God. If some more general relation to God made a sin one against God, finding a different relation that is not so general that it applies to any sin whatsoever becomes difficult. For example, if explicitly striking at God is not what amounts to sinning against God but instead harming something that is part of God's creation, some particular sin would not warrant hell on the strong view, but rather any sin whatsoever. No matter what part of the created order one aims at harming, one is thereby aiming to harm something that is part of God's creation. So, if some particular sin is to be singled out, it would seem to have to be a sin in which God is the explicit object of the wrongdoer's intention.

Defenders of the equal punishment version of the strong view will find little comfort in the restrictive view of sinning against God, however. The view that every person has at some point explicitly aimed at harming God or struck out at God in some way or other is difficult to sustain. In an age of growing atheism and agnosticism, some people may go through their entire lives never giving God much thought at all. Yet according to the equal punishment version of the strong view, all people headed for hell, whether they have given thought to God or not.

Because of this difficulty, the most common defense maintains the general view about sinning against God, according to which all sin is against God, regardless of who or what the explicit object of (actual or intended) harm is. Thus, once we note that this defense of the equal punishment version of the strong view must somehow bring God into the picture in order to have any chance of success, the conclusion toward which we are driven is that God is part of the picture in virtue of all sin being against him. So, we have three claims to investigate in considering whether the equal punishment version of the strong view of hell can be adequately defended by the "guilt proportional to status of offended party" principle. The first two matters discussed previously concern how to understand the notions of function and status involved in the principle, and the third concerns the defense of the claim that all sin is against God. Let us begin with this last claim.

Is All Sin Against God?

The most complete defense of the claim that all sin is against God was presented by Jonathan Edwards and recently endorsed by William Wainwright.[9] According to Edwards, all human behavior is either sinful behavior or truly virtuous behavior. True virtue consists primarily in "love to being[10] in general,"[11] and secondarily a relish of, or a delight in, the intrinsic excellence of benevolence.[12] God, for Edwards, is to be identified with "being in general"; "God is infinitely the greatest Being," "the foundation and fountain of all being and all beauty . . . the sum and comprehension of all existence and excellence."[13] If God is preeminently real in this sense, one cannot consistently identify true virtue with benevolence toward being in general and yet "insist on benevolence to the created system in such a manner as would naturally lead one to suppose" that it is "by far the most important and essential thing."[14] In summary, "a determination of mind to union and benevolence to a particular person, or private system, which is but a small part of the universal system of being . . . is not of the nature of true virtue" unless it is "subordinate to benevolence to being in general."[15] Hence, no person is truly virtuous who is not governed by a love of God and a delight in God's beauty.

Sinful behavior, according to Edwards, results from attachment to private systems (such as individual persons or groups) as opposed to benevolence to being in general. Because God is either identical with, or inextricably involved in, being in general, it follows that all sin is against God, which is the Edwardsian position.

This argument illustrates the features central to any argument for the claim that all sin is against God. First, sin must be described so that it involves aiming at something different from, perhaps opposed to, loving and being devoted to God. Second, one must claim that the proper goal of human conduct intrinsically involves loving and being devoted to God. From these claims it follows that sinful behavior involves pursuing some goal distinct from one's proper goal. This claim alone does not imply the desired conclusion—that all sin is against God—so a mediating premise is needed to the effect that any behavior aiming at something other than love of and devotion to God constitutes behavior directed against God.

The most difficult part of this argument concerns the mediating premise. It might seem that one can sin against an individual only by "aiming at" or "striking at" that individual, by having that person in mind as the intended object of harm. This position, however, is mistaken. For example, suppose we were to give away all of our money to some charitable cause, thereby ignoring our responsibilities to our children. In such a case, we might say that we sinned against our children by giving to the charitable cause, even though we had no direct intention to harm our children when we gave the money away. If our children did not have a legitimate claim on us for support, we would not have acted against our children by giving all our resources to charity. (One does not act against the Muscular Dystrophy Association by giving to the Crippled Children's Fund, for example.) When a legitimate claim is present, however, an action can amount to an action against an individual or group of individuals in spite of no harmful intent. For example, if I am obligated to help the starving in Africa, then my eating German chocolate cheesecake at my favorite restaurant with the money I ought to give to feed the starving in Africa may amount to an action against those starving people.

So we have no reasons stemming from some supposed intentionality requirement on sinning against someone to question the possibility of an argument to the conclusion that all sin is against God. There are, however, problems with Edwards's particular account of the matter. Consider a particular case of action: Joe, seeing a small child about to fall off a swing, responds in such a way that the impending accident is avoided, and his motive is compassion for the child. According to Edwards, this seemingly virtuous act is not completely virtuous unless Joe's commitment to the child is "subordinate to benevolence to being in general." Thus, unless Joe is governed by a love of God and a delight in God's beauty, saving the child from falling is, contrary to appearances, a tainted act; on Edwards's view, not only is all sin against God but also many good actions turn out to involve sinning against God as well.

This conclusion is mistaken. To perform a proper action from a good motive is one thing, and quite another thing is having a flawless character. We may grant that Joe's character is flawed if he does not love God and delight in God's beauty. Flaws of character, however, do not infect every action a person performs. A dishonest person can perform a flawlessly good act of charity; a callous person can, without a hint of fault, fulfill his obligation in a court of law by telling the whole truth and nothing but the truth. If Joe does not love God and delight in God's beauty, that is a character flaw, but holding that it infects every action he performs is implausible. In the case at hand, we cannot to hold that it infects Joe's action of saving the child from falling. As the story is told, the particular action is morally exemplary—he saves the child out of compassion.

I proclaim no view about a related position. Some moral philosophers hold that the virtues are one, in that to have any one virtue a person must have them all, at least to some degree.[16] This view encounters serious difficulties, for a person could be, for example, courageous and yet not compassionate. Whether such apparent counterexamples are decisive need not concern us here, however, for even if the unity thesis can be maintained, it cannot rescue Edwards's position, which is even stronger than the unity claim about the virtues. His position requires not just that one cannot be compassionate without being truly virtuous but also that one cannot perform even a single, morally untainted compassionate action without displaying true, complete virtue. To hold that having any virtue requires having them all is one thing; it is quite another to think that none of our actions can be untainted unless we are truly virtuous.

In sum, Edwards's argument is flawed because it counts some perfectly good actions as sins against God. But, of course, a defense of the claim that all *sin* is against God is not committed to the claim that all *behavior* (whether good or bad) by those not committed to God is sinful in some respect. The point here is that defending the claim that all sin is against God requires us to look elsewhere than to Edwards's argument, which is defective.

In the end I will counsel abandoning the strong view of hell and any defense of it by the status principle, but the basis of this counsel is not to be found in the present arena. Instead, I think an adequate argument can be developed to show that all sin is against God. This argument relies on the claim that our most fundamental obligation is to God and therefore any sin is a sin against God. Whether such an argument is adequate depends on what sense we attach to the term 'fundamental'. If 'fundamental' means 'most important', the argument is hopelessly defective: My obligations to my wife are more important than those to my horse, yet it does not follow that I would have sinned against my wife if I abused my horse. The sense required for the argument is this: an obligation is fundamental just in case all other obligations are derived from it. In this sense, to violate any obligation is to violate one's fundamental obligation.

Despite some complexities here, there is a natural line of argument for thinking that our fundamental obligation is to God. Because God is the creator and sustainer of all that exists, to behave improperly toward any of creation is to behave improperly toward God's handiwork. In the human case, to mistreat what another has made is not always to violate any obligation to that person (as, for example, when X mistreats what Y has created after purchasing it from Y), so it does not follow that all sin is against God merely because God is the creator of everything. Yet, in other cases mistreating the creation of another is to wrong that individual. In order to determine whether mistreating God's creation involves sinning against God, we need some idea of when mistreating the creation of another violates an obligation to the creator and when it does not. Although I cannot state precisely how to draw this distinction, it has to do with intimacy and immediacy of relationship. Someone who harms an infant wrongs not only the infant but the infant's parents as well, and the explanation has to do with the intimate connection between parent and child. This immediacy and intimacy of relationship are not merely biological; when a mother gives up her infant for adoption, the primary caretakers then become wronged when the child is wronged.

Although this appeal to intimacy, immediacy, and connectedness is quite vague, it is nonetheless something at the heart of our moral experience. Some relationships are morally significant ones, so that wrongs done against one partner in the relationship constitute wrongs done against the other partner as well. We might label this phenomenon the "transitivity phenomenon": some relationships are such that when A wrongs B and B is related to C in an appropriate way, A wrongs C as well. The question is what relationship causes this transitivity phenomenon to occur. My answer is that the appropriate relation has to do with intimacy, immediacy, and connectedness. This answer would be excessively vague if our interest were in the phenomenon of transitivity itself. For our purposes, however, a vague answer is sufficient in that whatever more precise answer one might develop, the most intimate, the most immediate, the most connected relationship possible is exemplified in the relation between God and creation. According to theistic conceptions of the universe, God not only created all that is but also sustains everything at every instant of its existence. Thus, however we might make the appeal to intimacy, immediacy, and connectedness more precise, no such investigation could cast doubt on the fact that, in sustaining the created order, God is a participant in the phenomenon of transitivity; that is, God's relation with the created order is so direct and intimate that any wrongs done against it count directly as wrongs done against God. Hence, all sin is against God.

The catch to this argument is the doctrine of divine conservation, the claim that God sustains the universe at every instant of its existence. This doctrine is controversial and, should it prove untenable, a distance would be introduced between God and creation so that mistreatment of God's creation would no longer clearly amount to sinning against God. After all, one might claim, because God is no longer involved in creation, God no longer is in an immediate enough relationship to the created order to undergird the phenomenon of transitivity. By way of analogy, wrongs against children might be seen as wrongs against their parents, but only as long as the parents are responsible for and caring for their children. Once a child becomes an adult and moves away from home, mistreatment of that person may anger the parents, but it does not amount to wronging the parents.

I am not sure whether this objection can be overcome, should the conservation doctrine have to be abandoned. We need not pursue that line here, however, because we have, I think, a decisive argument that the conservation doctrine should not be abandoned.[17] One ordinary way of avoiding the conservation doctrine is by suggesting a watch–watchmaker analogy: God's relation to the universe is like that of a watchmaker to a watch he builds, winds up, and puts aside to let it run "on its own." He need not constantly manipulate the gears to keep the correct time; instead, a mark of being a good watchmaker is that the watch is fully functional on its own.

This analogy is defective to the core. What allows the watchmaker to make a watch that works without his continued involvement in its operation is the structure of the universe the watchmaker uses to his advantage in order to secure the continued operation of the watch. The watchmaker relies on the physical constituents of the universe and the physical laws governing bodies, including the watch he is making, to keep the watch working when the watchmaker ceases his activity. In the case of the relation between God and creation, there is no third thing, the structure of which God can exploit in order to secure the continued operation of the universe, should God's activity cease. Because, in Christian theology, God is the creator of all that is distinct from God,[18] any explanation of the continued operation of the universe must appeal to either God or the universe itself, and nothing like this is present in the watch–watchmaker case.

This difference between the two cases cuts to the heart of the matter. In that, according to Christian theology, nothing exists besides God and creation, for the conservation doctrine to be false, God's creation would have to have the property of self-sustenance built into it. To have such a property would require special relation between what God creates and its (continued) existence. In order to show the necessity of God's continual conservation of the universe, we need only consider what this property of self-sustenance might be thought to be like. Properties come in two kinds: Some are essential to the thing that has them, so that the thing cannot exist and lack the property in question; others are contingent or accidental to the thing that has them, so that the thing in question has them but might exist without them. Note first that the property of self-sustenance cannot be essential to God's creation. If the property of self-sustenance is essential to a thing, then that thing cannot exist without bearing some special relation to its continued existence. Yet nothing can bear any kind of relation to its continued existence without continuing to exist! So the very fact that God could destroy the universe shows that neither it nor anything in it has the property of self-sustenance essentially.

So if anything can have the property of self-sustenance, it could have it only contingently or accidentally. In this conception, God made a decision at creation whether to grant the property or not, and until a thing ceases to have the power to sustain itself, it continues to exist. The difficulty with this position is that it does not avoid the need for the conservation doctrine. To see the problem, note first that, if this property is accidental or contingent, we need some explanation not only of creation's originally having the property but also of its continuing to have it. Perhaps it acquired the property when God created it, but that provides no assurance that it will continue to have it and does not explain why it has it at any future time.

One might claim here that its continuing to have the property of self-sustenance is simply a continued effect of God's original creative act. Here the breakdown with the watch–watchmaker analogy is crucial. Without some "medium" to carry the effects of an action at one time to a later time, no sense can be attached to the notion of a later effect of an earlier action. We are able to perform acts that have effects at later times because the universe is so structured, causally and temporally, that intervening events enable our actions to have consequences after the actions themselves cease. For example, lighting a match on Tuesday can be causally responsible for a forest fire on Friday. The way such things happen is for a series of overlapping events to occur, each of which is bound to its immediate predecessor and successor by the laws of nature. To continue the example, the lighting of the match causes it to burn, and its burning causes a leaf or blade of grass to begin to smolder, and so on. In the relationship between God and creation, no such structure is available to carry the force of God's original decision to a realization at some later time. There are no laws of nature independent of God and to which God is answerable in creating. The laws of nature are true because of God's creative activity. Hence, the only sense to be made of God's actions having later effects is in terms of the divine resolve to ensure that the original decision be carried out *by carrying it out* at the later time. We cannot protest that, once the causal medium that governs the universe is in place, God can exploit it to make certain that the force of the initial creative act will be carried through to later times, in the sustenance of the things God creates. God can exploit it *only by also sustaining the medium itself.* This alternative is of little comfort; God's sustenance of the universe still occurs at every instance of its existence, in this case through sustaining the medium that serves as a means to the goal of the sustenance of things.

So the conservation doctrine must be accepted. If it is, we can demonstrate that all sin is against God. Our fundamental obligation arises from the relationship that exists between God and us, and any sin results from missing the mark of loving God and delighting in God's beauty. At times, this sin may occur by the conscious rejection of God in favor of other things, but the ordinary occurrence would seem to be that of harming or intending to harm other things. Because God is the author and sustainer of the existence of all that is, such wrongdoing counts as wrongdoing both against the created order and against God.

Thus what might have seemed to be the most problematic of the three claims essential to supporting the strong view of hell is defensible. The two remaining issues concern the status and function aspects of the moral principle under consideration. I turn first to the status aspect.

The Issue of Status

As we have seen, the equal punishment version of the strong view of hell requires that the wrongness of an action is a function not only of actual and intended harm but also of the status of the individual who is the object of the action. This emphasis on status immediately raises the question of how status is to be determined. Some rankings make the status principle obviously false. For example, we could rank beings by weight, height, or longevity. Less ridiculous, although still inadequate, would be to rank beings according to their social status, so that killing a prince would be more serious than killing a serf in feudal societies.[19]

As noted, these rankings are obviously inadequate to the principle in question because, given these rankings, the status principle is false. However, other rankings hold more promise. One such ranking classifies beings according to individual characteristics such as moral character or dignity. According to this interpretation, the status principle claims that the wrongness of an act depends not only on the amount of actual and intended harm but also on the moral character or dignity of the one harmed. Although this principle appeals to a ranking system that is more plausible than those considered in the last paragraph, Marilyn Adams argues that the status principle is false even on this interpretation.

> Suppose that Schweitzer and Gandhi are equally saintly and that Green and White are equally unsavory characters with long criminal records. Suppose that on separate occasions Green gratuitously slaps Schweitzer in the face, Schweitzer gratuitously slaps White in the face, and Gandhi gratuitously slaps Schweitzer in the face. If guilt were proportional, not just to the offence, but to the moral uprightness of the offended party, then Green would incur more guilt and liability to punishment than would Schweitzer. For since Schweitzer is worthier than White, Green's failure to show respect for Schweitzer was more grievous than Schweitzer's failure to show respect for White. Similarly, Gandhi's action would be more culpable than Schweitzer's. In fact, I think we are more apt to consider guilt as directly proportional to the nature of the offender than to the nature of the offended party. Schweitzer's action in slapping White is, if anything, more culpable than Green's action in slapping Schweitzer. In view of Schweitzer's long-standing habits of self-control and moral

behaviour, we should expect more from him than from Green who has never developed these habits. Similarly, we should expect more from Gandhi. Nor would we say that Gandhi's act was more culpable than Schweitzer's. We might even have some inclination to be less outraged at Gandhi, since he was at least 'picking on someone' of his own moral stature.[20]

Adams claims that more is morally required of a person the better that person is. In the example she cites, more is demanded of Schweitzer and Gandhi than of Green and White, who have never developed the moral character of Schweitzer and Gandhi. The status principle under the proposed interpretation is false if Adams is right, for it ranks the disvalue of a slapping in terms of the moral character of the one slapped. If she is right, the moral character of the one slapped is not important, but rather the moral character of the one doing the slapping.

Adams's argument also considers only ranking in terms of moral character and not in terms of dignity. However, the same difficulties that plague a ranking system in terms of moral character plague a ranking system in terms of dignity. In too many cases seriousness of wrong does not depend on individual characteristics. Robbing a store run by a man who beats his wife is just as wrong as robbing the store of a virtuous saint, and torturing a pauper is just as wrong as torturing a prince. These claims are subject to a *ceteris paribus* clause, however, for in special cases slapping Green, for instance, is of a different moral status than slapping Gandhi. For example, if Green is slapped because of his villainous nature and Gandhi is slapped because of his saintly nature, the slappings are no longer of the same moral status. The explanation of the difference, however, need not appeal to either Green's or Gandhi's character. Instead, it should appeal to the difference in the intentions of the person slapping: To slap for being a villain involves a different intention than to slap for being a saint. The second is worse than the first, not because Gandhi has a better character than Green, but rather because holding saintliness against people is worse than holding villainy against them.

This problem for the status principle—that ordinary cases of wrongdoing do not depend for their seriousness on traits of the particular victim—is an instructive problem. The lesson of the difficulty is that our ranking of status is too fine-grained. If we rank beings in terms of height, weight, longevity, moral character, or dignity, our ranking system makes more distinctions than the status principle can absorb and it is rendered false. The lesson, then, of these difficulties for the status principle is that the ranking system needs to be coarser if we are to find a true interpretation of that principle. Moreover, the particular reasons the fine-grained approaches fail suggest what a coarse-grained approach must look like. The problem with the fine-grained approaches is that they do not treat all human beings equally, contrary to our moral understanding.

These considerations suggest that any adequate account of status must be coarse enough that all human beings count as having the same status. The question we must ask, then, is whether an adequate coarse-grained account of status with this implication exists. What we need is an account of how status is determined that implies, for example, that all human beings are of the same status, but all bipedals are not. This example is instructive in that a natural response would seem to be that, when we divide the created universe at natural points of division, we end up with humans in one category and nonhumans in another; to divide the created universe into bipedals and nonbipedals does not "carve nature at its joints." So we treat all humans alike in virtue of the fact that they all fall into the same natural kind; we do not treat all bipedals alike because they do not all fall into the same natural kind.

Whatever our attitude toward this particular account of our moral practice of favoring human beings over, say, chickens, this account is instructive regarding what an acceptable coarse-grained account of status should look like. This line of reasoning suggests that the way we generate equality of treatment for some range or collection of beings is on the basis of some underlying metaphysical commitment regarding the arrangement of the universe into natural (and supernatural) kinds. If we could develop an adequate account of what kinds of things there are, we could formulate a status principle in terms of this metaphysical construction. Furthermore, this metaphysical construction offers some hope for a ranking of these kinds into more important and less important from a moral point of view. At the very least, the metaphysical construction provides conceptual input for the ranking task; it supplies the concepts that must be ordered into more important and less important. So, if the ranking task cannot be completed, the fault does not lie in this way of formulating the status principle. Finally, if we could complete both tasks—categorizing things into kinds and ranking these kinds relative to each other—perhaps an adequate account of status would be forthcoming. That account would claim that, all else being equal, harming or intending to harm a member of a higher ranked kind is worse than doing so to a lower ranked kind. Wainwright proposes just such an interpretation of the status principle in defending Edwards's argument that all sin is against God, against Adams's counterexample concerning the slappings among Green, Gandhi, Schweitzer, and White.

> The principle in question is not clearly false if it is restricted to differences in ontological kinds and not applied to differences between more or less valuable members of the same ontological kind. For consider the following series of actions—destroying a flower, destroying a dog, destroying a human being, and destroying an archangel. Each action in this series appears to be intrinsically worse than its predecessor (presumably because human beings, for example, are a more valuable kind of thing than dogs). But a restricted principle is all we need since God is a unique kind of being, and the value of the relevant kind ("divinity") infinitely surpasses the value of other kinds.[21]

Wainwright's position in this passage exemplifies the strategy counseled previously for defending the status principle. The account of status it employs is metaphysical; it claims that individuals differ in status only if they differ in kind-membership, and they differ in status just in case one of them is a member of a more valuable kind than the other.

One way to follow this strategy is as I suggested before: Carve nature at its joints and then rank the resulting kinds in terms of moral value. In the passage quoted, Wainwright suggests a version of the principle in accord with this strategy, for he explains the killing of various kinds of beings in terms of the natural kind to which they belong. He also suggests a more restrictive approach as well. He says all that the defender of the status principle needs to do is to divide kinds of beings into two categories, divine and nondivine. He notes that the value of any divine being infinitely surpasses the value of any nondivine being and for this reason concludes that this version of the status principle is correct and can help to rescue the equal punishment version of the strong view of hell from the moral objection to it.

This approach to the status principle, which counts kind-membership as an important moral factor in determining the seriousness of wrong, deserves serious consideration, for it is the best account developed so far for defending the status principle. Moreover, it is the only defense of that principle that seems to have any chance at all of being adequate. Nonetheless, the value of any such defense of the principle depends heavily on the selected principle of division among kinds of beings. In particular, Wainwright's latter suggestion concerning how to divide beings into kinds should be rejected. This suggestion is that the status principle need countenance only two kinds of beings, divine and nondivine. Whether Wainwright is correct in this judgment depends on the context of inquiry. In a context of attempting to formulate a status principle against which no persuasive counterexample can be forthcoming, Wainwright is correct. The present context, however, places more strenuous demands on the division of beings into kinds, for the feature of the equal punishment version of the strong view that is subject to objection is that the equal punishment version assigns such a severe punishment to even the slightest sin. This objection does not become any less forceful when we grant that, in sinning, we all sin against God as well as against other individuals. In this context, Wainwright's restrictive principle looks like question-begging, for it says merely that sins against God are infinitely more disvaluable than sins against anything else. Yet, that is the precise implication of the equal punishment version of the strong view against which the objection is raised. To anyone not already convinced that this version of the strong view of hell is not morally objectionable, this defense amounts to nothing more than question-begging.

There is another reason to be dissatisfied with the more restrictive principle. The source of our discussion of the status principle has to do with the foundational features of morality, with what features of a situation, at bottom, determine the moral significance of an action. The restrictive status principle, however, is not the kind of principle appropriate to an explanation of the foundational features of morality. If it is true, it appears to be just the kind of moral truth that can be true only by virtue of following from some more general moral truth. For example, suppose someone suggests that one fundamental feature of what makes an action right or wrong is whether it causes me pain. The proper response is that my pain is a morally relevant feature, but it is certainly not a fundamental feature. Rather, it is a morally relevant feature because it is a fundamental feature of morality that *anyone's* pain is morally relevant. Just so, if the restrictive status principle is true (that all else being equal, harming or intending to harm a divine being is more serious than doing so to a nondivine being), it is a truth only by virtue of following from some more general moral principle. In the present context, this restrictive principle is useful to the equal punishment version of the strong view of hell only if it is derived from the more general status principle, which makes reference to the division into kinds that results from carving nature (and supernature) at its joints.

So if the status principle is to be employed to defend the equal punishment version of the strong view of hell, it cannot be given the restricted interpretation that the only kind distinction it attends to is the distinction between divinity and nondivinity. Instead, the more general interpretation, which pays attentions to a broader range of kind differences, has to be employed. The claim is, then, that one constituent in an adequate response to the moral objection to the equal punishment version of the strong view of hell is that seriousness of wrong depends not only on harm done and harm intended but also on which kind one's action is directed toward, where the relevant kinds include all the natural division within the created universe (i.e., natural kinds) and, of course, supernatural kinds and any divisions there might be among them (e.g., demons, angels, divine beings). Moreover, this emphasis on status must be irreducible; there must not be a way to derive this principle from more fundamental moral principles that do not appeal to the status of the object of actual or intended harm in determining the moral status of an action.

I believe that this interpretation of the status principle cannot be sustained. In summary form, I will argue that the principle faces a dilemma in responding to certain objections to it. If no response is given, a reasonable conclusion to draw is that the principle is false. The only response available, however, makes the principle impotent for use in a response to the moral objection to the equal punishment version of the strong view, for the response requires that the status of the object of actual or intended harm is not an irreducible component in evaluating the moral status of an action.

The argument for these claims concerns what properties or characteristics of a thing explain how it ought to be treated. For example, suppose that all animals have a right to life, but nothing else does. Further, suppose that, strange as it may sound, every animal is bigger than a breadbox and no nonanimal is as big as a breadbox. We could then formulate a moral principle that encountered no actual counterexamples: All else being equal, killing anything bigger than a breadbox is wrong, killing anything smaller than a breadbox is permissible. No one following this moral principle would ever actually do anything wrong, but that fact is uninteresting because the property of being bigger than a breadbox is not the right kind of property to appeal to in explaining what behavior is proper. Just what kinds of properties are the right kind is controversial. Even so, some pro-

posals deserve attention and others do not. A theory that claims that
being sentient is morally explanatory is a proposal that deserves
attention; a theory that claims the same for being four-legged is not.

One might be tempted to think that these considerations reduce
to the question of whether a proposed moral principle is immune to
possible counterexample. If a principle implies that an action is
wrong when directed at a thing having property P, then property P
might be thought to be morally explanatory just in case there are no
possible counterexamples to the principle. This view of the matter is
mistaken. Suppose property R is morally explanatory regarding killing (perhaps R is sentience), and further suppose that property P is
logically although not conceptually coextensive with R; that is, suppose it is logically impossible for anything to be P and not be R or to
be R and not P, but that it is possible for a person to conceive of
either P or R without conceiving of the other. Because explanatory
relations are not constant under substitution of logical equivalents,
we have no reason to suppose that morally explanatory relations are
constant in this way. For example, suppose classical theism is true,
according to which God's existence is a necessary truth. In such a
case, the truth of the statement that God exists would explain the
falsity of physicalism, but the truth of the statement that $2+2=4$
need not, even though, under the assumptions, the statements *God
exists* and $2+2=4$ are logically equivalent. Just so, not every moral
principle immune from counterexample is a morally explanatory
principle, for not all logically coextensive properties are equally explanatory of the moral status of certain actions.

In the context of the ontological kind account of status, the
important question is whether being a member of a certain kind is
morally explanatory. Consider Wainwright's example about killing
a plant versus killing a dog. Wainwright says that the explanation of
why the second is worse than the first is in part because a dog is a
more valuable kind of thing than a plant. If so, perhaps we should
conclude that the property of being a dog is morally explanatory
regarding the wrongfulness of killing things that have that property.

Surely, however, this conclusion is strongly counterintuitive. If
anything explains why killing a dog is worse than killing a plant, it
will have to be a property other than that of being a dog. Perhaps, for
example, it is worse to kill a dog than a plant because dogs are
sentient beings and plants are not. For those yet unconvinced, I
think there is a good argument to show that the property of being a
dog is not morally explanatory. Consider the legacy of the Cartesian
philosophy that nonhuman animals, including dogs, are only com-

plex machines. Much of our knowledge of the gross anatomical features of animals comes from vivisection after this element of Cartesianism became popular, vivisection done without the aid of anesthetics. These researchers (many of them nuns in convents) may not all have been wicked and perverse individuals, or at least their wickedness and perversion need not have extended beyond their culpability for accepting the Cartesian philosophy! They thought the animals were not experiencing anything at all, and their remarkable displays of painlike behavior witnessed instead to the miraculous power of a deity capable of making a machine to mimic real pain. How could such individuals engage in this research? The obvious answer is that the properties of things that are morally explanatory with regard to how they are treated are not ontological kind properties. It is not by virtue of a thing's being a dog, for example, that explains why it should not be carved alive with no anesthetic. Instead, it is by virtue of being sentient that dogs deserve not to be treated in this way. The Cartesian researchers need not have been confused about morality, or wicked, perverse, or in any other way morally deficient. We can explain their behavior completely by noting merely that they were in the grips of a bad philosophy. They missed the connection between being a dog, for instance, and being sentient. Most important, they need not have been confused about which of these properties is morally explanatory regarding what kind of treatment a thing deserves.

Wainwright can grant this objection, abandon the ontological kind account of status, and still employ the status principle to respond to the moral objection to the equal punishment version of the strong view of hell. Earlier, we saw that dividing ontology into the divine group and the nondivine group is too coarse-grained to be of service to the strong view. We have now seen that the ontological kind account of status is too fine-grained, for many sentient things fall into different kinds. The strategy a defender of the status principle should follow, then, is to find an account of status somewhat more coarse-grained that the ontological kind account, yet more fine-grained than the scheme with only two groups of beings, the divine ones and all the rest. Instead of appealing to the hierarchy of kinds to explain why some actions are worse than others, the appeal is made to a principle that orders nature at a more general level.

Unfortunately, however, this approach cannot be entirely successful. The problem is that, by moving to a more coarse-grained account of status, one risks losing the needed distinction between actions aimed at God and actions aimed at other individuals. For example, if all sentient beings are of the same status, the status principle no longer implies that sinning against God is worse than sinning against your brother. Here the virtue of the ontological kind construal of status becomes clear, for it is fine-grained enough that the distinction between sin against God and sin against one's brother is easily maintained. The objection to such a construal is that the ontological kind of which an individual is a member is not a *morally relevant* fact about it. If this objection is granted and one begins substituting a more coarse-grained account of status that does appeal to morally relevant facts, then one no longer has any guarantee that the distinctions that need to be preserved in order to rescue the strong view of hell can be preserved.

The severity of this problem can be seen by noting what properties beyond sentience seem to be morally explanatory. Perhaps, for example, being a person is a morally relevant property that distinguishes a subclass of sentient beings as deserving special moral consideration. For example, it is worse to kill a sentient individual than a nonsentient one, and it may also be worse to kill a sentient being who is a person than a sentient being who is not a person. These moral distinctions may be based on a particular value theory, according to which pain is intrinsically bad and persons are intrinsically valuable.

This division still does not generate the conclusion that sinning against God is worse than sinning against one's brother, so some further division is called for if the status principle is to be of any use in salvaging the strong view of hell from the moral objection to it. Of course, an immense array of facts about God signal his vast superiority to us and his measureless importance over ours, but that any of these facts are morally explanatory ones is simply not clear. God is more important than we are because everything depends for its existence on him, but that fact does not explain why sin against him is worse than sin against one's brother. God is perfectly good and essentially so, but degree of perfection in moral character is not morally explanatory either. If it were, then killing a saint would be worse than killing a nonsaint, and it is not (all else being equal). In sum, for any of the countless ways God is superior to us, it is simply not obvious that these superiorities can establish what a defender of the equal punishment version of the strong view of hell needs.

We can gain further insight into this difficulty by considering how one might attempt to argue that sentient persons have a different moral status than sentient nonpersons. Animal rights advocates argue that no relevant difference can be found, and they may be right. If they are wrong, however, the difference would seem to have something to do with the conceptual capacities of human beings. Perhaps the capacity to conceive of their entire lives and form plans and goals for them—and how death destroys not only the individual but also the possibilities of future happiness and fulfillment at having achieved such life plans—is a morally significant factor. Alternatively, perhaps having the ability to form and follow moral maxims is itself a crucially relevant moral factor, or having the ability not only to be in pain but also to be self-consciously aware that one is in pain (assuming a distinction can be drawn here) is morally significant.

Such accounts are the kinds that defenders of the status principle must give respecting the difference between divine and nondivine persons if they are to provide a reasonable account of why this distinction is significant from a purely moral point of view. The difficulties I have been raising suggest that any of the overwhelming number of differences between divine and nondivine persons will not be useful to this task. Although we should not underestimate the differences between God and us, none of the intrinsic characteristics of divinity as opposed to humanity seems capable of sustaining this response to the moral objection to the equal punishment version of the strong view of hell.

Lest I be misunderstood, let me point out a morally significant way in which God is distinguished, according to Christian theology. As noted earlier, in the Christian view as in other theistic views, everything that exists owes the entirety of its being to God, both in terms of origination and sustenance. So, in some sense, it follows from this doctrine that we owe everything to God and clearly do not owe everything to anything else. This morally significant fact, however, establishes only that the morality of all of our actions must be judged in part in terms of what we owe to God. In effect, nothing we can ever do fails to involve our creator. This point, however, affects only the extent to which God is a part of our lives. It shows that God's involvement in our lives is unlimited from a moral point of view. It explains the *extent* to which our actions are related in a morally significant way to God, but that is insufficient for use in a defense of the equal punishment version of the strong view of hell by the status principle.

So no construal of the status principle is adequate to the needs of this defense. Some cautionary remarks are in order, however, about how strongly I intend my argument to be taken against the status principle, for the previous discussion does not demonstrate—and I

am not claiming—that this principle is false or even that the equal
punishment version of the strong view of hell actually is morally
objectionable. Instead, all that can follow is that a defense of the
doctrine of hell employing the status principle fails to satisfy some
apologetic constraints on an account of hell. I do not wish to take us
on a lengthy detour of what an adequate apology for the Christian
faith must be like, and doing so would not be profitable, given the
purposes of this work. Nonetheless, some general remarks on the
matter can clarify the way in which the discussion of the strong view
of hell should be taken. An adequate apology for the Christian faith
should provide the means for a non-Christian theist fitting the legal
notion of "the reasonable man" to avoid irrationality in coming to
accept that Christianity is true. Most especially, irrationality should
not arise in coming to accept the basic picture Christianity claims
holds between God and humanity. Exactly what constitutes this
"basic picture" is controversial, but, as I have argued, one crucial
aspect of it concerns the doctrine of hell. To make any sense at all of
the purpose of God in Christ, we must have some account of the
destiny of humanity apart from this work. Hence the doctrine of hell
that Christians accept is subject to conditions of apologetic adequacy, and on this criterion the strong view is inadequate. Critics of
the equal punishment version of the strong view of hell can fit the
legal notion of "the reasonable man," and yet we have found it
extremely difficult to formulate a moral principle such a person can
accept that accounts for the severity of hell on this version of the
strong view. To put it succinctly, no known principle is adequate to
the required task.

It is in the weak sense of inadequacy that this defense of the
equal punishment version of the strong view of hell by the status
principle should be found wanting. It is not inadequate because of a
decisive argument against it. No such argument exists because there
are avenues to explore open to those inclined toward this version of
the strong view where an adequate response to the moral objection
might be found. In particular, some explanation might be forthcoming as to why the class of persons should be divided into divine and
nondivine subclasses for purposes of determining the moral status of
actions against such individuals. This task is not easy, and I do not
see how it can be accomplished. In fact, I believe that it cannot be
accomplished, but I have given no argument to show that. So all we
are entitled to conclude at this point is that no account of status is
available that can serve to alleviate the moral problem for the equal
punishment version of the strong view of hell.

The Equal Seriousness of All Sin and Punishment Deserved

The final issue to be addressed concerns which function on status and harm caused is appropriate for determining the moral disvalue of a wrong action. For this purpose, let us suppose that some version of the status principle can escape the difficulties raised in the previous section. The important question, if we grant this point, is what function on action and status is appropriate for determining the seriousness of a wrong action. In particular, the issue is whether the right function on status and harm caused implies that even the most insignificant wrong considered in itself can be infinitely disvaluable when committed against God. In order to justify the equal punishment versions of the strong view of hell, a nondiscriminatory principle about wrongdoing must be implied by a proper construal of the function aspect. According to this principle, the distinctions among the seriousness of wrongs considered in themselves can disappear if the wrong is done against God.

Wainwright gives an example that concerns treating a person with mockery or ridicule versus lying or committing a minor theft, when done against a "good and holy" person. The point of the example is to show that "in cases in which the dignity of the person against whom an offense has been committed is very great, the offense is quite grave even though the act which constitutes it is comparatively insignificant when considered by itself, and causes little or no harm."[22] Such examples are useless in the present context in that they rely on a version of the status principle according to which status is determined by the moral character or dignity of the individual. We have seen that such a version is inadequate, and no example relying on such an account of status can aid in determining which function on status and action is appropriate.

Furthermore, even if the example did not rest on an unacceptable account of status, it would be of little use in the present context. We need some defense of the nondiscriminatory principle about wrong done against God. Most worrisome for defenders of the equal punishment version of the strong view is that a distinction must be drawn between sin against God and sin that "aims at" or "strikes at" God by virtue of having God as the intentional object of the intended harm. Even though all sin is against God, there is nonetheless a difference between determining which individuals have been wronged by one's actions and determining the seriousness of the wrong for purposes of punishment. To conclude that all sin is against

God only shows that God is wronged by every instance of sin. In order to assess the seriousness of the wrong done, attention must also be paid to the intentions of the wrongdoer, for wronging a person is one thing and intending to wrong that person is quite another. We are more lenient in cases of weakness of the will than in cases of deliberate wrongdoing precisely because of the difference in the intentional realm in the two cases. In cases of weakness of the will, the person in question is overwhelmed or overinfatuated with the good-making characteristics of a wrong action; in cases of deliberate wrongdoing, the person consciously chooses to violate a known obligation. Deliberate wrongdoing involves a flouting of one's obligations that weakness of the will does not. In cases of deliberate wrongdoing, the violation of the obligation falls under the intention with which the person acted; in cases of weakness of the will, it does not.[23]

These facts give us reason to distinguish among a variety of aims a person might have in sinning against God. The intention least connected with God occurs when the person has never considered the claims of deity on his or her life and sins against God unawares. Such a case can be either a case of deliberate wrongdoing or a case of weakness of the will. So there are at least two kinds of wrong action:

(1) A wrong action involving no thought of God but involving an intention to actualize some good-making characteristic of a wrong action, and

(2) A wrong action involving no thought of God but involving an intention to actualize a wrong action in its wrongness.

Stronger types of wrongdoing occur with an awareness of God. They fall into two further categories. There is, on the one hand, the mere personal awareness of God and that what one is doing is displeasing to God. Such an awareness has no particularly moral content, and, as such, this type of an awareness displays, according to Christian theology, a confusion concerning the concept of God. In that theology, God is worthy of worship and his commands have the characteristic bindingness of moral demands; these features are not mere incidental features of God, but are central to the very concept of God.[24] So, beyond the mere personal awareness of God is a stronger awareness of God, on the other hand, one that involves conceiving of God as worthy of worship and as one whose desires, wishes, and commands place moral requirements on us. Let us call the first type of awareness a 'clouded awareness of God' and the second type a 'perspicuous awareness of God'. Each such awareness can be connected with wrongdoing either through weakness of the will or deliberate wrongdoing, so at least four more possible wrong actions must be considered.

(3) A wrong action involving a clouded awareness of God and an intention to actualize some good-making characteristic of a wrong action,

(4) A wrong action involving a clouded awareness of God and an intention to actualize a wrong action in its wrongness and in opposition to the desires of God,

(5) A wrong action involving a perspicuous awareness of God and an intention to actualize some good-making characteristic of a wrong action, and

(6) A wrong action involving a perspicuous awareness of God and an intention to actualize a wrong action in its wrongness and in opposition to the moral demands arising out of God's desires.

These distinctions reveal a deep problem for the nondiscriminatory principle central to the equal punishment version of the strong view of hell. Surely (6) deserves a much more serious punishment than does (1), even if the wrong done in each case is infinitely bad in an objective sense because both are against God.

A defender of the equal punishment version of the strong view of hell might attempt to respond to this objection by citing differences in wrongs in our legal system that are not matched by differences in punishment. For example, whether a person is a mass murderer of fifty people or five people, the punishment is not any different (assuming the number killed is the only difference in the two cases). Just so, there may be gradations from (1) to (6) without any implication concerning gradations of punishment. If (1) deserves the punishment that follows according to the equal punishment version of the strong view of hell, then (6) surely does as well even though (6) is worse than (1).

This response is not satisfactory, however. Any version of the strong view of hell assumes a completely retributive account of why a person ends up in hell. On such an account, the only relevant characteristic for determining the appropriate punishment is the fit between the punishment and the crime. In order to sustain the response of the last paragraph, the defender of the equal punishment version of the strong view must hold that the fit between capital punishment and ordinary murder is the same as the fit between capital punishment and mass murder. Clearly, however, that is not the case. Whatever punishment is fitting for ordinary murder, a greater punishment is fitting for mass murder.

Why then does our society punish each the same? One reason is that our penal system is not based on a completely retributive theory of punishment. It also takes into account reform and deterrence. A second reason concerns who might impose such punishments if we were to impose the demands of a completely retributive theory of punishment. Ordinary humans would suffer from being the instruments of such punishment. Some of the suffering would arise perhaps out of guilt for having one's own wrongdoings go unpunished. More important, however, is the concern that we become what we do. If we torture people before killing them in order to ensure that they receive their just deserts, we risk coming to appreciate the torturing itself. In the end, perhaps only the thoroughly callous and sadistic would be able to hold such jobs. Clearly, we should not have a penal system that encourages such character traits.[25]

So we fail in attempting to salvage the equal punishment version of the strong view by pointing out that mass murderers receive the same punishment in our penal system as do ordinary murderers. Our system does not assume the theory of punishment assumed by the strong view, and hence what it does is irrelevant to that view. Equally important is the fact that our system must balance the legitimate retributive concerns against the social costs of imposing the punishment that fits the crime. Note that this factor does not affect God's punishment, on the traditional theistic conception. His moral character is completely and wholly untainted and immutable, so that God never needs to balance the demands of justice against the costs to his character in imposing the punishment. God could impose a punishment only because it was demanded by justice; he could never degenerate as we can to the point of inflicting punishment for its own sake or for the sake of the suffering that results.

Hence the equal punishment version of the strong view of hell cannot escape the difficulty raised by the distinctions among cases (1) through (6). Even though sinning against God may be infinitely bad, it does not alter the fact that (1) deserves a less severe punishment than does (6).[26] Perhaps an analogy would be helpful in assuaging any residual concerns. Being responsible for the death of another human being is one of the worst things one can do regarding a human being, objectively speaking. Yet the objective disvalue of being responsible for the death of another human being is not the only factor that determines whether any punishment is due and what that punishment should be. Such responsibility includes cases of mere causal responsibility, cases of negligence, cases of intentional but not premeditated murder, and cases of premeditated murder. What punishment is due depends both on the objective evaluation of what was done and on a subjective evaluation of the intentions of the agent in doing what was done. Just so, even if all sin is against God, this is not the only factor in determining what punishment is deserved, for different intentional components are possible.

The nondiscriminatory principle therefore must be abandoned. With it goes the defense of the equal punishment version of the strong view of hell against the moral objection, for we have found no acceptable moral principle to which a defender of the strong view of hell might appeal in order to respond adequately to the moral objection. No acceptable version of the status principle implies that sin against God is worse than sin against other persons, and even if sin against God is worse than sin against any other, the nondiscriminatory principle is still false. Hence the equal punishment version of the strong view of hell cannot be rescued from the moral objection to it.

The Arbitrariness Problem

The strong view of hell faces another problem that will be increasingly important throughout this work. Because it is independent of the moral problem, it is worth mentioning at this point. Suppose, contrary to what I concluded previously, that the equal punishment version of the strong view of hell could be defended against the moral objection to it. In other words, suppose an argument showed that it is morally permissible to send someone to a hell as imagined by the defenders of this version of the strong view. Even if the view were unobjectionable in this way, that God could send someone to this kind of hell would not follow. To have reason to believe that God could send someone to hell, one's picture of hell must be something more than a picture arbitrarily selected from a gallery of alternatives, one among a host of alternatives from which one randomly selects in developing a complete theology. This requirement can be misunderstood easily, so I will attempt to make it plainer.

Once a general account of hell is accepted, there will be a multitude of ways to instance it, just as there are a number of ways to construct a house, given a set of plans for it (by using pine or fir lumber, for instance). A general account of hell must say enough so that hell and heaven are exclusive and exhaustive of the (ultimate)

afterlife possibilities, and it must say enough to rule out objectionable interpretations (one does not build a house of balsa wood, even
if pine or fir would be equally adequate). In order to address the
arbitrariness problem, however, something more is needed. Some
reason is needed to think that the resulting doctrine is true, and
providing such a reason results in a picture of hell in which the
doctrine of hell incorporated into one's theology is no longer merely
arbitary. Simply arguing for the moral acceptability of the strong
view of hell fails to address these issues, for no reason has yet been
given for thinking that this conception of hell is anything more than
one possibility on equal epistemic footing with many other alternatives that also survive moral scrutiny. We might call this problem
"the arbitrariness problem" because it arises when certain claims
about the afterlife are left untreated, creating the impression that a
theology has elements to it that are arbitrary.

Before examining the arbitrariness problem in more detail, considering some objections to my characterization of that problem is
important. Everyone will agree that any account of hell that portrays
the doctrine as a completely arbitrary accompaniment of one's theology is inadequate, but not everyone will agree that one can avoid
the arbitrariness problem only if one's account implies that heaven
and hell are exclusive and exhaustive alternatives in the afterlife. We
might wonder how the doctrines concerning purgatory and limbo fit
in here, as well as about the possibility of a synergistic combination
of Christian and Eastern thought so that the Christian view of the
afterlife is supplemented with a doctrine of reincarnation. Before
examining the relationship between the arbitrariness problem and
the strong view of hell, defending my characterization of that problem against these objections is important.

First, my characterization does not rule out the possibility of
purgatory, but it does rule out the claim that purgatory is an intermediate state between heaven and hell. Yet the doctrine of purgatory
is not best understood as an intermediate state, even though this
language is sometimes used. In that no one goes from purgatory to
hell, purgatory is best conceived of as a part of heaven (although not
perhaps as enjoyable as other parts of it). Moreover, residence in
purgatory is temporary; one stays in purgatory only as long as is
demanded by the character and extent of one's offenses (or, perhaps,
by one's need for character development). So purgatory is not a separable, ultimate possibility in the afterlife distinct from both heaven
and hell.

Furthermore, I do not mean to rule out the possibility of reincarnation. By 'afterlife', I mean to refer to what is true about the times after one's earthly life or lives are over. I happen not to believe in the possibility of reincarnation, but the doctrine of the afterlife is, as I see it, strictly irrelevant to that issue. If reincarnation could and did occur, it would either be endless, in which case there would be no afterlife (or, more accurately, "afterlives"), or it would end at some point, when the doctrine of the afterlife would come into play.

The most difficult of the objections raised to my characterization of the possibilities in the afterlife arises out of the doctrine of limbo. According to some branches of Christian thought, limbo is the place where virtuous pagans and unbaptized infants go in the afterlife. If such a possibility exists, then the alternatives of heaven and hell are not jointly exhaustive of afterlife possibilities.

I do not believe, however, that there is any good reason for such a doctrine. The temptation toward such a doctrine arises from a very severe conception of hell combined with a very restrictive conception of how it is possible to achieve heaven. Once these conceptions are in place, discomfiture is bound to arise from considering the plight of certain individuals implied by these accounts. The proper lesson to learn here, however, is not that of an afterlife possibility in addition to heaven and hell, but rather a disjunctive one. Either one's conception of heaven and hell is inadequate, or the discomfiture one experiences is misleading about the moral acceptability of certain individuals ending up in hell. On the first option, the problem is best dealt with by developing an adequate theology of heaven and hell, one immune from the problems that engendered the desire for a doctrine of limbo. On the second alternative, one should explain why no objection to sending such individuals to hell can withstand scrutiny. In such a case, the discomfort certain folks feel at the thought of virtuous pagans, for example, ending up in hell is just another case of a relatively common phenomenon. Sometimes the truth hurts, sometimes virtue has its cost, and sometimes justice requires actions that have regrettable aspects. So, the proper response to the objection arising from the doctrine of limbo is that positing such a doctrine is a clear sign that one's theology of heaven and hell is inadequate: Either the doctrine defended is inadequate, or the defense needs some work. I maintain, then, that any account of the afterlife that posits some ultimate state of individuals other than heaven or hell is inadequate, and any account of the afterlife that does not characterize the afterlife in such a way that heaven and hell are exclusive and exhaustive of the afterlife possibilities is subject to the arbitrariness problem.

Any view of hell that is morally objectionable will succumb automatically to the arbitrariness problem, for no such an account can be defended against any alternative, morally adequate account. The opposite, however, is not the case. Even if the strong view of hell were unobjectionable on moral grounds, it still might face the arbitrariness problem. Even if it would be morally permissible for God to send some persons to hell, that it would be impermissible for him, for example, to give them a second chance at redemption does not follow.

As the next chapter shows, responses can be made on behalf of the strong view of hell as to why the typical alternatives to it are inadequate. Even if the usual alternatives can be eliminated, however, the arbitrariness problem still remains. To solve it, one must be able to provide some positive reason for thinking that a particular conception of hell is true. Merely showing that typical alternatives to a particular conception are inadequate fails to constitute such a positive reason. Furthermore, those who defend the strong view give little indication as to where such a reason might be found, and there is, I think, an instructive reason why this is so. The primary historical influences on the development and sustenance of the strong view of hell as the orthodox conception of hell are literary in character. They include Jesus' parable about the rich man and Lazarus, Dante's *Divine Comedy*, and Milton's *Paradise Lost*. Such representations of spiritual claims have a strong psychological impact because of their literary character, but the price of this virtue is the weakness of literary vehicles for the expression of abstract truth. A piece of fiction is not well suited to the task of explaining why its particular figural arrangement is alone correct among the alternative stories that might be told. Such figural presentations are immensely valuable for producing indelible mental images of what one wishes to convey, but pictorial representations of doctrine cannot of themselves account for why that version of the doctrine, as opposed to its competitors, represents things as they are. Because the strong view of hell has found a natural home in figural presentations and no natural literary home in the style of the treatise, it is quite vulnerable to the arbitrariness problem independently of its vulnerability to the moral problem.

A word of explanation is in order about my claim that a solution to the arbitrariness problem requires some reason for thinking that one's preferred view is more likely to be true than its competitors. In particular, one may wonder why it is not sufficient only that one's view is *as likely* as its competitors. The weaker standard may be appropriate if we were inquiring concerning the rationality of individuals who accept a particular version of the doctrine of hell. To be rational may require only that one's view stands up to the evidence as well as any other view, but the task we are considering is the theoretical task of providing a philosophically adequate theology of Christianity. In approaching that task, I have argued that a conception of hell is crucial. Any such conception can be more or less specific, and by being more specific a conception of hell faces competitors that more general conceptions do not face. For example, the strong view of hell, as I have outlined it, is not committed to any literal elements involving fire and brimstone, although such views count as instances of the strong view. Had we addressed the more specific view that is committed to literal flames in hell, such a view would have to face competitors that the strong view, as clarified, need not address because they are instances of it.

Given this distinction between more general and more specific accounts of hell, we can think of various accounts of hell as forming a branching tree structure; each account of hell branches off from a node above it that represents another account of hell of which the more specific account is an instance. Any two theories on the tree structure can be counted, then, as being at the same level of specificity if they branch from nodes of the same level of generality. Now suppose a theologian is considering incorporating an account of hell of level n into a theology, and that account is recognized as no more likely to be true than some other accounts of the same level. What is the reasonable approach in such a case? I submit that the reasonable thing for such a theologian to do is to try to move to more general accounts of hell, of which the account in question is an instance until one is found that has no competitors that are equally as likely to be true. If such a more general account can be found, that account ought to be affirmed and not the more specific versions that cannot be defended against competitors.

In the one case such a strategy fails, moving to more general accounts of hell fails to produce an account superior to all competitors. In such a case, no matter how general one's account gets, one cannot provide any reason for thinking that the preferred account is superior to its competitors. In such a case, I suggest, the proper theoretical stance is a skeptical one: Admit that no doctrine of hell has solved the arbitrariness problem and that a proper approach to that doctrine is a disjunctive one that describes alternatives that are equally likely to be correct. One can also maintain that, should one find oneself believing one of the doctrines and disbelieving the rest, one might still be rational; what is rational to believe and what is proper to commit oneself to in the process of theory construction are different subjects. I submit that, whereas failing to lose to the competition may be sufficient for rational belief, it is not sufficient for a complete and philosophically adequate theology.

The arbitrariness problem can arise for the strong view in another way as well, in addition to arising by virtue of the inability to find a reason for thinking that it is more likely to be true than its competitors. The strong view has no resources to explain why heaven and hell are exhaustive of the possibilities in the afterlife. This problem is important in the contemporary context, for, as noted in the introduction, one quite strong contemporary attitude toward hell treats it as a piece of Hollywood fiction, on par with the interestingly outlandish pieces of science fiction that abound in our culture. The reason for this problem is what we might call the "geographic" orientation of the strong view of hell, which is again a by-product of the figural vehicles by which the strong view has come to have the hold it does on traditional Christianity. It treats heaven and hell as places on a cosmic map where God will send one, depending on one's spiritual state at death. This geographic orientation is intrinsically problematic, for heaven and hell are not places on a map, but rather the only possible alternatives for the afterlife. Instead of such a geographic orientation, one needs a metaphysical or logical orientation toward the subject, in the sense that the heart of the doctrine of heaven and hell concerns the logical or metaphysical possibilities beyond the pale of earthly existence. Without such a metaphysical orientation, the fictionalizing of hell in the minds of nonbelievers will be a continuing irritant to those who take the doctrine seriously.

In sum, then, the equal punishment version of the strong view is deeply problematic. It succumbs to the moral objection to it, and it is also susceptible to the arbitrariness problem. This final problem would have plagued the view even if it were morally unobjectionable. So, for a variety of reasons, we should look for an alternative conception of hell.

Other Versions of the Strong View

The equal punishment version of the strong view of hell is, however, only one version of the view, and failing to consider alternative ways of affirming the strong view would be unfair. Of two possibilities we need to consider here, the first maintains that the description of hell provided by the strong view is only a contingent view, and that the problems the equal punishment version of the strong view encounters arise only when it is construed as having a stronger modal status. According to this view, hell just *happens to be* as the equal punishment version of the strong view claims it is; the problems with the doctrine discussed before are then claimed to arise only because it is assumed that hell *must be* as the equal punishment version claims. The second possibility maintains that the strong view of hell can be supplemented by differentiating among the eternal punishments received in hell. Let us consider the contingency claim first.

A Contingent Equal Punishment Version of the Strong View

The contingent modification maintains that hell is as the equal punishment version claims, not because God established it to be that way necessarily, but because human beings have so acted, and are disposed to act, that the nature of hell is as that version maintains. In essence, the contingent view holds that all humans, at some time or other, intentionally and maliciously strike at God in their actions and thereby deserve the sort of punishment described by the equal punishment version of the strong view of hell. Although such punishment can fail to be deserved, as a matter of fact, it is deserved; although sinning against God is possible without deserving the punishment described by the equal punishment version of the strong view, as a matter of fact everyone sins against God in just the way sufficient to deserve the most serious punishment.

This modification of the equal punishment version of the strong view is unsatisfactory even if it is true. If hell just happens to be as this version of the strong view maintains, then this version is derived from a more basic conception of hell. If a more basic conception exists, we would do well to attempt to understand it, for the equal punishment version is not rationally convincing, and the only way to remedy this problem is to probe deeper into the problem of hell.

There is another way to put this point. As I have already argued, an adequate theory of hell must contain elements that explain why it is the only final afterlife alternative to eternity with God. Otherwise, a view will have been offered that cannot be defended against alternatives, for the theory will not be able to rule out the possibility of a third option of neither heaven nor hell. If it cannot be defended against such alternatives, the theory has to cast as an arbitrary de-cree the decision of God to constitute the afterlife according to the theory. The difficulty I am raising for this modification of the equal punishment version of the strong view in terms of its modal status is that it has no resources to explain why there are two and only two ultimate possibilities in the afterlife. So, even if this modification generates a correct view, it does not provide an adequate answer to the problems with the equal punishment version of the strong view of hell.

The Differential Punishment Version of the Strong View of Hell

The second modification of the strong view holds that by virtue of the fact that all have sinned against God, an infinite punishment is deserved. Nonetheless, it claims, there are different types of infinite punishments. Those who sin against God, unaware that they are doing so, get a less severe punishment; those who sin deliberately, having a perspicuous awareness of God, get the most severe punish-ment. Eternal consignment in a minimum security prison is not nearly so bad as eternal consignment in a medieval torture chamber. Just so, hell is thoroughly eternal, and yet the punishments meted out are not all the same.

This view does not escape the moral problem. The nature of punishment deserved is not a simple function of the degree of dis-value of the wrong done. If it were, we would have to punish anyone guilty of causing the death of another person with at least life im-prisonment. Yet we do not and should not do so, for the intentions of the individual are of critical importance in determining the punish-ment due. If the death was an accident, perhaps no punishment is due. If the death was premeditated, a severe punishment is due.

This version of the strong view of hell ignores the importance of the intentional realm for assigning punishment. Instead of consult-ing the intentional realm from the beginning of the process of assign-ing punishment, it refers to the intentional realm only after the basic sentence has been assigned. This procedure is totally unwarranted. The intentional realm must be consulted in order to determine what sentence is justified; if the person was blameless at the intentional level, no degree of disvalue of the act in question can license a very severe punishment, if any punishment at all.

So whereas the equal punishment version of the strong view of hell failed in that it did not distinguish punishments according to differences in the intentional realm, this differential punishment version fails in that it ignores the intentional realm when assigning a basic sentence for a wrong done. On the contrary, the intentional realm is intrinsically involved in determining what sort of basic punishment is due.

In addition, this version of the strong view does nothing to address the arbitrariness problem. Even if hell involves different types of punishment for different individuals, the view is still plagued by an inability to explain why heaven and hell are the only ultimate afterlife possibilities. This defect can be traced to the same source as other versions of the strong view, for the primary vehicles for conveying this account of hell are fictional, with the inherent limitation of fostering a geographic—as opposed to metaphysical—conception of hell. Figural presentations of theology are inherently *particular*, whereas any solution to the arbitrariness problem must arise at a level of generality that discusses the range of logical possibility. This emphasis on the particular is the fundamental difficulty of geographic conceptions of hell. They ignore the need to consider the entire range of logical possibility and focus instead on particular possibilities and landscapes. Regardless of how psychologically forceful such presentations can be, there is simply no alternative to a theoretical treatment of doctrine when the issue of truth arises.

Conclusion

So, the strong view must be abandoned as an adequate account of the nature of hell. This conclusion is problematic for Christianity because this view is the traditional doctrine of hell. In the next chapter, however, I argue that matters are even worse. The typical alternatives to the strong view, which I call "simple alternatives," are developed by dropping commitment to one of (H1)–(H4). Each of the simple alternatives is at least as problematic as the strong view itself, and this fact shows that whether any account of hell can be a component of an adequate theology of the Christian religion is far from a settled issue. The remainder of the work then focuses on how to escape this dilemma—an apparently unacceptable traditional doctrine and at least as unacceptable alternatives, and the problematic character of Christianity apart from a doctrine of hell. First, however, we must investigate alternatives to the traditional doctrine.

Notes

1. Medieval theologians distinguished between the pain of loss (*poena damni*) and the pain of sense (*poena sensus*); the first referred to the loss of

the *visio dei* and the second to some actual suffering of those in hell. The tendency in Christianity has been to conceive of hell in terms of both kinds of pain, but it has never been a matter of orthodoxy to so conceive it.

2. The scriptural basis used to support this doctrine is found in 1 Peter 3:18–20a, which reads in the New International Version, "For Christ died for sins once for all, the righteous for the unrighteous, to bring you to God. He was put to death in the body but made alive by the Spirit, through whom also he went and preached to the spirits in prison who disobeyed long ago when God waited patiently in the days of Noah while the ark was being built." Protestant theology has consistently resisted the "harrowing of hell" interpretation of this passage. For example, Oliver Buswell says, "In the interpretation of these verses I follow the teaching Charles Hodge, B. B. Warfield, A. T. Robertson and others in understanding that the time when Christ preached to the persons who were, in Peter's day, called 'Spirits in prison,' was 'in the days of Noah,' and that Christ preached in the Spirit through Noah who was called a 'preacher of righteousness'" (2 Peter 2:5) (*A Systematic Theology of the Christian Religion* [Grand Rapids, 1962], 2:319). According to Buswell, Christ preached in the Spirit through Noah and at the time of Noah. The preaching was not between Christ's death and resurrection, as it is according to the doctrine of the harrowing of hell.

3. For discussion of this issue, see Philip Quinn, *Divine Commands and Moral Requirements* (Oxford, 1978); and Paul Helm, ed., *Divine Commands and Morality* (Oxford, 1981).

4. This moral principle must be relativized to context, for considered as an absolute requirement, it implies that neither dropping the bomb nor invading Japan is justified. In order to use the justification suggested in the text, one must first assume that the war itself was just, so that the only remaining question is what means could be justified for ending the war. In that context, the moral principle cited can be used without implying that neither dropping the bomb nor invading Japan is justified. Note also, however, that the moral principle can only succeed in justifying dropping the bomb if the facts to which it appeals actually obtain. Dropping the bomb is justified by this principle only if, in fact, lives are saved by so doing.

5. The moral principle that might be thought to justify hell because of harm caused is the "eye for an eye" principle. Marilyn Adams has examined several interpretations of this principle (in "Hell and the God of Justice," *Religious Studies* 11 (1975); 433–447; and "Divine Justice, Divine Love, and the Life to Come," *Crux* 13 (1976–1977), 12–28), and concluded that no interpretation is successful in defending the justice of the strong view of hell. Her reasons are the same as those I give in the text.

6. The moral principle that might be used to justify hell on the basis of intended harm is the "to will it is as bad as to do it" principle. Aquinas defends this view. He suggests that one reason in favor of the strong view of hell is that "'before the divine seat of judgment the will is counted for the deed,' since 'just as man seeth those things that are done outwardly, so doth

God behold the heart of men' (I Kings 16:7)" (Thomas Aquinas, *Summa Contra Gentiles*, Book III, part 2, ch. 144, translated by Vernon J. Bourke in *On the Truth of the Catholic Faith*, Book III, part II (Garden City, 1956), pp. 215–216; quoted in Adams, "Hell," p. 444). Aquinas goes on to give a bad argument employing this principle. "Now, he who has turned aside from his ultimate end for the sake of a temporal good, when he might have possessed his end throughout eternity, has put the temporal enjoyment of this temporal good above the eternal enjoyment of the ultimate end. Hence it is evident that he much preferred to enjoy this temporal good throughout eternity. Therefore, according to divine judgment, he should be punished in the same way as if he had sinned eternally. But there is no doubt that an eternal punishment is due to an eternal sin." As Adams notes, the fallacy here is that it does not follow from the fact that one wills some X that entails Y that one has willed Y. For example, Oedipus can will the death of the stranger on the road without willing the death of his father, even though the stranger is his father, and so the death of the stranger entails the death of his father.

7. Some may be inclined to argue that condemnation to hell need not be justified by any actual sins a person commits, but can be justified solely by the doctrine of original sin. Space does not permit the detour needed to discuss this view, but the intransigent moral problems for this position are not difficult to see. Such a position, instead of solving the moral problem, merely bites the bullet on it. For a useful discussion of the issues surrounding the doctrine of original sin, see William Wainwright, "Original Sin," *Philosophy and the Christian Faith*, Thomas V. Morris, ed. (Notre Dame, 1988), pp. 31–60.

8. The distinction between mortal and venial sins is irrelevant here. The difference between these kinds of sins concerns what requires damnation if not forgiven and what requires only finite suffering in purgatory. This does amount to a difference in the seriousness of some sins, but is not in any way relevant at this point. Even given this distinction, the issue still remains whether one mortal sin or more than one would be needed to justify the eternal punishment as described by the strong view.

9. William Wainwright, "Original Sin," *Philosophy and the Christian Faith*, Thomas V. Morris, ed. (Notre Dame, 1988).

10. Edwards thinks of being as conscious being.

11. Jonathan Edwards, *The Nature of True Virtue* (Ann Arbor, 1970), p. 4.

12. Ibid., p. 3, 11.

13. Ibid., pp. 14–15.

14. Ibid., pp. 16–17.

15. Ibid., p. 18.

16. This view derives from Plato. For a discussion of Plato on the unity of the virtues, see Terence Irwin, *Plato's Moral Theory* (Oxford, 1977).

17. For a more complete defense of this doctrine, see Jonathan L. Kvanvig and Hugh J. McCann, "Divine Conservation and the Persistence of the

World," in Thomas V. Morris, ed., *Divine and Human Action: Essays in the Metaphysics of Theism* (Ithaca, N.Y., 1988), pp. 13–49. For more on the connection between the doctrine of divine conservation and the philosophical position of occasionalism, see, by the same authors, "The Occasionalist Proselytizer: A Modified Catechism," in James E. Tomberlin, ed., *Philosophical Perspectives 5: Philosophy of Religion, 1991* (Atascadero, Calif., 1991), pp. 587–616.

18. For a defense of this view of creation, see Thomas V. Morris and Christopher Menzel, "Absolute Creation," *American Philosophical Quarterly* 23 (1986), pp. 353–362.

19. Adams notes that Aquinas cites this feature of feudal society in discussing the moral principle in question, and she also correctly notes that nothing in Aquinas's argument actually depends on this feudal practice. See Adams, "Hell," p. 442.

20. Ibid.

21. Wainwright, "Original Sin," pp. 34–35.

22. Wainwright, "Original Sin," pp. 34–35.

23. This discussion of the distinction between deliberate wrongdoing and weakness of the will covers over a multitude of complexities. For one thing, the phrase 'in opposition to' is ambiguous: Read one way, it covers cases of wrongdoing in which a wrong is done for the sake of its wrongness; read another way, it covers cases of wrongdoing that involve only doing a wrong for the sake of something else, although still intending that the wrongness be realized. Pursuing these complexities is not to the point here; all I wish to do is to point out that even when someone intentionally does something wrong, the severity of punishment deserved hinges on the particular content of the intention.

24. This claim does not imply that any sort of divine command theory of morality is correct. According to a divine command theory of morality, obligations are to be explained in terms of what God wills or commands: We have such obligations because God wills or commands the content of the obligation. If a theology affirmed such a theory, it would have a ready explanation of why God's commands create moral demands, but a divine command theory is not necessary for the truth of the claim that God's commands create moral demands.

25. It can even be argued that the penal system we have corrupts those who participate in it. If so, perhaps the best way to think of the justification of a penal system is in terms of some attempt to balance the corruption of those who staff it with the well-ordering requirements for a decent social system.

26. We have a chance later to consider an expansion of the strong view of hell on which, even though the punishment for every sin is infinite, some infinite punishments are more severe than others.

2

Simple Alternatives to the Strong View

So far, we have seen several versions of the strong view of hell that are inadequate, and the kinds of problems these versions have encountered suggest that no version of the strong view can be acceptable. In response to this problem, the simplest path might seem to be to delete one of (H1)–(H4), the theses that in combination yield the strong view, from one's account of hell. This approach maintains an intellectual economy of effort; it can presuppose the fundamental picture of hell maintained by the strong view and yet hope to give an account that avoids the difficulties plaguing that view. As we shall see, the most common alternatives to the strong view result from dropping one of the theses of that view, thereby lending support to the suggestion that within the strong view is to be found, in the terminology of Imre Lakatos,[1] the "hard core" of a research program aimed at finding an adequate solution to the problem of hell. Such alternatives to the strong view are what I call "simple alternatives." In arguing that all such views are inadequate, I begin with the two that can be dismissed most easily, the alternatives that deny the Existence Thesis and the No Escape Thesis, respectively. After completing an investigation of all simple alternatives to the strong view, I will suggest why the defects with simple alternatives, combined with the results of the last chapter, show that the approach to the problem of hell shared by both the strong view and its simple alternatives is, again in Lakatosian terminology, a degenerative one. That is, the assumption is false that one can find within the strong view of hell a hard core that represents the proper approach to solving the problem of hell.

On Abandoning the Existence Thesis

The view that denies the Existence Thesis we can call "the annihilation view." Such a theory still maintains (H1), the claim that some
people end up in hell, (H3), the claim that no one can leave hell once
there; and (H4), the claim that the reason for hell is to mete out
deserved punishment. What it denies is that any persons exist in
hell. Instead, hell is the condition of nonexistence. That is, 'hell' is a
term that denotes what becomes of a person whom God literally
annihilates.[2]

The problems for the annihilation view are the very same ones
that plagued the strong view in the last chapter. Nothing is to be
gained in responding to objections to a penal theory by substituting
metaphysical capital punishment for metaphysical life imprisonment; if anything, our views about capital punishment would suggest that the annihilation view assigns a more severe punishment
than does the strong view. So if the strong view cannot offer an
adequate response to the moral objection, neither can the annihilation view; if the strong view cannot solve the arbitrariness problem,
neither can the annihilation view.

These problems with the annihilation view are quite obvious,
yet surprisingly it has been perceived over the last few centuries as a
mitigation of the strong view of hell.[3] One explanation of this delusion is that the annihilation view is being contrasted with a view of
hell involving the literal language of fire and brimstone. To some,
defenders of the strong view might seem to conceive of hell in terms
of torture, and God ought instead simply to annihilate persons rather
than torture them. In times past, preachers and theologians have
contributed to this misperception of the essence of the strong view.
Many of them believed that the moral fiber of society depended on
the doctrine of hell to such an extent that the more horrific the
doctrine could be portrayed—even if the preacher or theologian took
the portrayal to be inaccurate—the greater its deterrent power
against wrongdoing.[4] In the seventeenth and eighteenth centuries,
for example, when religious tolerance was broadening, this new tolerance was generally considered not to extend to atheists and Socinians because of the impact such tolerance would have on society.
Atheism and immorality were highly associated to such minds, and
Socinians were dangerous in the same way because they believed in
the annihilation of the wicked.[5] Here, then, we find a historical
example of two important points to be stressed in understanding
why the annihilation view is perceived as a mitigation of the strong

view. First, appropriate representations of hell were constrained by the perceived demands of public morality so that exaggerations of the strong view are quite common in the history of Christian thought; second, the annihilation view was perceived to present greater, even intolerable risks of turning well-ordered society into an anarchical orgy as compared with common exaggerations of the strong view.

This sociological thesis about the connection between immorality and the doctrine of hell is controversial, but I will not pursue that topic here. Regardless of the merits of this view, any religion is in an uncomfortable position when it feels compelled to offer a lie in service of the public good.[6] Even worse are the prospects for an adequate defense of any version of a religion depending on such a lie. More important in the context of an evaluation of the merits of the annihilation view over against the strong view is the point that nothing in our discussion of the strong view commits it to any picture of hell involving literal fire or brimstone; the problems facing the strong view have nothing to do with imagining hell in terms of a torture chamber of any sort. Hence, attempting to deal with the difficulties plaguing the strong view by resorting to the annihilation view is ineffective even if the annihilation view has some privileged position with respect to a torture chamber image of hell. Once we distinguish clearly between the philosophical core of the strong view and figural accretions to it, we can easily see that the annihilation view is completely impotent in solving the problems facing the strong view of hell and, in particular, in no sense involves a mitigation of the strong view.

A defender of the annihilation view might respond to these charges by claiming that I am confusing two distinguishable views here. One might claim that my objections are sound when applied to the view according to which God actively destroys individuals, but those same objections are not sound when applied to the view that individuals are only conditionally immortal. According to this latter view, God need not do anything in order for a person to fail to exist in the afterlife, for no person is intrinsically immortal. Instead, the realm of God's activity is to be found among those in heaven. God makes some persons immortal by intervening in the course of things, which is toward nonexistence. So even though holding that God intervenes to destroy some individuals would be problematic, holding that he merely fails to intervene in order to preserve in existence certain individuals is not problematic. Just like the significant moral difference in the human realm between killing and let-

ting die, there is a significant moral difference between the annihilation view when it construes annihilation as requiring the active
intervention of God to destroy life and the annihilation view when it
claims only that God fails to intervene so as to preserve life. The first
view might be more appropriately thought of as annihilation by way
of commission, whereas the second is better put in terms of annihilation by way of omission.

This attempt to rescue the annihilation view by distinguishing
two versions of it fails because it does not take into account the
doctrine of divine conservation. As we saw in the last chapter, every
created thing continues to exist only by virtue of God's continual
sustaining activity. Every created thing, that is, tends toward nonexistence, and only by God's power does anything that exists continue
to exist. If so, however, there is no distinction to draw between
annihilation by omission and annihilation by commission. Annihilation occurs whenever God fails to act to preserve a thing in existence. Whether this failure of preservation is labeled a commission
or an omission is not to the point; instead, the point is that no
distinction is to be drawn between commissions and omissions in
this context. Hence, there are not two versions of the annihilation
view to distinguish in hopes that one might escape the criticisms I
have been raising.

Once the lack of distinction between two kinds of annihilation
is appreciated, it becomes easy to see why the distinction between
killing and letting die, although important in some contexts, is not
relevant here. Given the doctrine of divine conservation, God is
intimately involved in our existence at every point in time, even
more so than a mother is involved in the continued existence of a
newborn. Furthermore, a mother would have no defense by appealing to the distinction between killing and letting die in an attempt to
absolve herself of responsibility for the death of a newborn through
neglect. So, once we give up the idea of a distinction between annihilation by commission and annihilation by omission, we should also
give up the idea that the distinction between killing and letting die
can make annihilation innocuous by analogy with cases of letting
die.

Even given the doctrine of divine conservation, there are distinctions between different possible holds on existence. Some things are
subject to corruption, to death or annihilation in virtue of the deterioration of their parts. Other things, if there be such (e.g., immaterial
souls, spirits, angels, and the like), are not subject to corruption.
That one that is not subject to corruption has the property of self-

sustenance does not follow, however. As I argued in the last chapter, nothing capable of destruction could have such a property, and hence no alternative exists to the view that every created thing— whether corruptible or not—continues to exist solely by virtue of the sustaining activity of God. If that is so, however, there is no distinction between the conditional immortality view, which wishes to picture annihilation in terms of omission, and some more strictly conceived annihilation view, which pictures annihilation in terms of commission. Only the one type of annihilation exists, and it is subject to the problems raised before. Hence, if a simple alternative to the strong view is to be found acceptable, we shall have to look elsewhere than at the view that abandons the Existence Thesis.

On Abandoning the No Escape Thesis

Another position that can be dismissed with dispatch is one that denies (H3), the No Escape Thesis. Of course, merely denying (H3) does not yield an acceptable doctrine of hell, for there are many suggestions about getting out of hell that are unacceptable to Christianity. For example, adding that one gets out by sinning even worse than one did on earth would be obviously absurd. The most plausible view, from a Christian perspective, would be the same way one might have avoided it in the first place. Views that deny the No Escape Thesis we can call "second chance theories of hell."

Regardless of the attractiveness of second chance theories, they do not solve the moral problem faced by the strong view of hell. If no adequate reply is forthcoming to the charge that an infinite punishment is not always deserved, second chance theories fail. If assigning a punishment of a particular duration to a person, would be wrong, then assigning that same punishment conditional on his or her not repenting would be wrong. To see this, consider a simple example. Suppose to cut off a thief's arm is unduly harsh in punishment for a crime. The sentence does not become appropriate to the crime if it is changed to the conditional sentence of cutting off one's arm unless one apologizes. The ease with which one can avoid a punishment does not guarantee a fit between punishment and crime. The only way to ensure a proper fit between punishment and crime is to offer an unconditional punishment appropriate to the crime.[7]

We might be tempted to disagree with these points about conditional and unconditional punishments. In disciplining our children, we often employ conditional punishments. For example, if our five-year-old has just hit his visiting cousin with a stick, we might say,

"If you don't apologize, you will have to go to your room," and our considered judgment, I agree, is that such a conditional punishment is perfectly appropriate. In such a case, however, the conditional punishment is appropriate because either recourse is adequate and justified in light of the behavior of the child: Either the child apologizes or the child is sent to his room. In order, then, to use such practices in defense of second chance theories, a defender would have to argue that either recourse involved in a conditional punishment is adequate and justified in light of the behavior in question. As we have seen, that requires relieving the strong view of hell of the moral objection against it, for it involves arguing that an infinite punishment is deserved by human wrongdoing.

Second chance theories come in two varieties, and this objection applies directly to only one of them. The other variety of second chance theory is discussed later, so some explanation is needed of the distinction in order to make clear this postponement. To see the distinction between the two types of second chance theories, we need to remind ourselves that historical Christianity divides a person's existence into three parts. The first part is one's earthly life, the second concerns what happens to one at death, and the third part involves one's eternal state after the final judgment. The second chance doctrine as outlined previously assumes that one consigned to hell at the final judgment goes there immediately upon death. The other variety of second chance theory claims that one goes to hell only at the consummation of all things, that is, at the final judgment. According to this latter variety of second chance theory, one's state between death and the final judgment may involve a preview of hell, but it is not hell itself.

We can then distinguish between second chance theories that posit a second chance after one has already taken up eternal residence in hell and those that posit a second chance after death but prior to consignment in hell. The first view we have discussed before, but the second view need not deny the No Escape Thesis. It might, instead, deny the Retribution Thesis. It need not deny that residence in hell is retributively based on what one has done in the past, but it would deny that the relevant past is only one's earthly past. Instead, according to this view, what justifies the eternal punishment of hell is the character of one's earthly life plus what has occurred between death and the final judgment at the consummation of all things. Discussion of this second chance doctrine is postponed until we examine alternatives to the strong view that deny (H4), the Retribution Thesis.

The important point in the present context is that no second chance theory constituted by a denial of the No Escape Thesis is successful in avoiding the problem of hell. However, one way of abandoning the No Escape Thesis lacks the problems faced by such second chance theories. Its difficulty is that it is not clear what connection exists between it and historic Christianity. One might simply hold that hell is just a divine—rather than earthly—prison to which persons are sent to serve time for their sins. Some verdict is reached in each case about the sentence deserved, and the person is incarcerated for the required length of time. Upon serving one's time, one is then released; where one goes is perhaps undetermined, but another sin would result in another period of incarceration.

This view of hell is not connected to Christianity in any significant way. In particular, it fails to be compatible with the eschatological dimensions of Christianity. Traditional Christian faith expects a final consummation of all things. This picture of hell is more akin to views that posit a cyclical or cylindrical order of events with no final consummation. A final consummation requires some account of what could or would happen to those who ultimately reject God. Because this account ignores this eschatological dimension of Christianity, it cannot be judged to be an acceptable solution to the problem of hell.

On Abandoning the Anti-Universalism Thesis

Probably the most popular solution to the problem of the moral objectionability of hell is universalism. Universalists deny (H1), the Anti-Universalism Thesis, and instead hold that all persons will in the end be reconciled to God. Universalist views, although traceable to the Alexandrian school of theologians founded by Clement and Origen, have become increasingly popular in the last three to four hundred years.[8] Although orthodoxy has never wavered since condemning universalism at the Fifth General Council at Constantinople,[9] a revival of interest in universalism began in the late seventeenth century with the Cambridge Platonists and carried into the eighteenth and nineteenth centuries in the work of Swedenborg, Tennyson, Kant, Schleiermacher, and Ritschl and in the rise of the Unitarian and Universalist denominations in America.[10] Universalism continues into the twentieth century, although the rise of the influence of existentialism clouds what might otherwise be a complete embrace by many of the most influential theologians of our century.[11] In addition, the demythologizing program of

Bultmann and the reinterpretation of salvation in terms relating to social, political, and economic affairs have all done their part both to undermine the traditional understanding of hell and to mask universalist tendencies. Those who take the afterlife and one's fate in it seriously, however, find universalism by far the most attractive view.

There are two importantly different versions of universalism (not always clearly distinguished even by defenders of universalism), and the prospects for each are not encouraging. *Contingent universalism* holds that, although a person could end up in hell as described by the conjunction of (H2)–(H4), as a matter of contingent fact every human being will end up in heaven. *Necessary universalism* holds that it is not only true but also necessarily true that every human being will end up in heaven; that anyone be damned is simply impossible.

Contingent Universalism

According to contingent universalism, the possibility exists that some people end up in hell, but as a matter of contingent fact, no one will. In the end, God's saving grace and power win out over the forces of evil, and the entire created order is redeemed. This position is quite common among contemporary theologians. One example is John Macquarrie.[12] His understanding of hell is in terms of annihilation; he says, "If heaven is fullness of being and the upper limit of human existence, *hell* may be taken as loss of being and the lower limit. . . . This utter limit of hell would be annihilation, or at least the annihilation of the possibility for personal being."[13] Given this understanding of hell, Macquarrie goes on to suggest a version of universalism: "If God is indeed absolute letting-be, and if his letting-be has power to overcome the risks of dissolution, then perhaps in the end . . . no individual existence that has been called out of nothing will utterly return to nothing."[14] To drive home his rejection of traditional conceptions of hell, he says, "Needless to say, we utterly reject the idea of a hell where God everlastingly punishes the wicked, without hope of deliverance. Even earthly penologists are more enlightened nowadays."[15]

So Macquarrie holds that the strong view of hell and its associates are at best unenlightened (elsewhere he terms such views "barbarous"), and that hell is best thought of in terms of annihilation (although the concept is a limiting one), in the realm of mere possibility at best, rather than the destiny of some human beings. Of special interest in the present context is the juxtaposition of universalism with the strong view of hell and its associates. This juxtaposition suggests the possibility that the inadequacies found in traditional conceptions of hell can be thought of as being overcome by a doctrine of universalism. We have already seen that annihilationism alone cannot solve the problems facing the strong view of hell, so if anything in Macquarrie's account can solve the problem of hell, it must be the affirmation of universalism.

Another influential and important contemporary theologian is Hans Küng, who summarizes his views about hell as follows:

> Hell . . . is to be understood theologically as an exclusion from the fellowship of the living God, described in a variety of images but nevertheless unimaginable, as the absolutely final possibility of distance from God, which man cannot of himself *a priori* exclude. . . . The eternity of the "punishment of hell" (of the "fire"), asserted in some New Testament metaphorical expressions, remains subject to God and to his will. Individual New Testament texts, which are not balanced by others, suggest the consummation of a salvation of all, an all-embracing mercy.[16]

Küng holds that even though existence in hell is a possibility, this dread possibility is only a mere possibility. In the end, the all-embracing mercy of God will overcome the grasps of hell in the consummation of a salvation of all.

Not only do a large number of theologians affirm universalism, but also an implicit theoretical motivation lies behind this affirmation, one having to do with the need to solve the moral problem of hell. This theoretical motivation can be found even in some of the more conservative Christian groups. In a recent issue of *Christianity Today*, Clark Pinnock, a conservative evangelical theologian, claims,

> If the doctrine of hell is taken to mean (as it so often is) that God raises up the wicked to everlasting existence for the express purpose of inflicting upon them endless pain and torment, universalism will become practically irresistible in its appeal to sensitive Christians. . . . If the only options are torment and universalism, then I would expect large numbers of sensitive Christians to choose universalism.[17]

Pinnock goes on to defend the annihilation view, but in the present context what is of greater significance is that he sees in universalism a solution to the moral problems facing the strong view of hell and its associates. According to Pinnock, if Christians face the options of a morally problematic view of hell on the one hand and universalism on the other, it would be fully understandable if Christians opted to embrace universalism.

This motivation suggests an argument for universalism that begins by pointing out the moral problem for traditional views of hell. The next premise claims that if no one were to end up in hell, the moral problem would disappear. The conclusion is then inferred that no one will end up in hell.

There are two defects to this argument. The first is a minor one, that the conclusion does not follow from the premises. At the very least, some additional premise is needed to the effect that no other adequate way solves the moral problem of hell. This premise is quite difficult to defend without a full and systematic investigation of the problem of hell, and no one has undertaken that task. So, as it stands, this argument for universalism is only as good as some as yet forthcoming full and systematic treatment of the problem of hell that can support the conclusion that universalism is the only adequate solution to the moral problem faced by traditional views of hell.

The second defect is more fundamental. In a word, this line of reasoning for universalism is confused. The difficulty is that universalism, even if true, fails to solve the problem of hell, for not only is God perfectly and wholly good in this world but also he would be perfectly and wholly good no matter what course affairs might take. He is not just contingently morally perfect; his moral perfection is essential to his character. As we have seen, there are severe problems with the strong view of hell, which show that sending anyone to hell would be wrong if this conception of hell were accurate. The suggestion made by those holding to contingent universalism does not change the conception of hell in question; it only holds that the census figures projected by some Christians are too high. Although such a move may eliminate a concern that God has actually done something wrong, it does nothing by way of defending his essential goodness and moral perfection. If it would be wrong to send someone to hell, it makes no difference to the inconsistency between God's sending someone to hell and his perfect goodness whether people end up in hell in the actual world or only in other possible worlds. According to contingent universalism, this irredeemably bad state of affairs does obtain in some (other) possible worlds. Hence, even if contingent universalism is true, it does not relieve us of the problem of hell. If hell is abhorrent, affirming contingent universalism will not solve the problem; it only modally masks it.

Necessary Universalism

If universalism is able to solve the problem of hell, then, it must do so in the form of necessary rather than contingent universalism. Yet, an argument against necessary universalism might seem as quick and easy as the one against contingent universalism. The argument I have in mind begins by asking us to recall that an essential commitment of Christianity is that we are all headed for hell apart from the redemptive work of Jesus. The argument then concludes by claiming that necessary universalism is committed to a denial of this claim. If no one can end up in hell, then Christ's work might seem superfluous.

A necessary universalist can, however, respond to this argument. A necessary universalist can deny the apparent superfluity of Christ's work by maintaining that it is impossible for God to fail to intervene on our behalf through the redemptive work of Jesus. In other words, the necessary universalist can avoid the charge of superfluity by maintaining that God could not have failed to send his Son and that his redemptive efforts through his Son could not have failed to be successful.[18]

So this first argument against necessary universalism is unsuccessful. A more damaging argument can be raised, however. It is the free will argument. In succinct form, it claims that God cannot guarantee the presence of all in heaven without being willing to violate the freedom of some individuals to choose otherwise. Fundamentally, this argument concerns the relationship between God's moral perfection and human free will. First, note that God's moral perfection, his holiness, requires his participation in the moral perfecting of fallen human beings. In particular, those who will be united with God for all eternity must become morally perfect (otherwise God would be either unconcerned about moral imperfection or unmotivated to help correct the defects, and either supposition is unbefitting an adequate conception of God.)

So if necessary universalism is true, no one can fail to be perfected, for such a failure is incompatible with God's holiness. Yet such conformance, it would seem, cannot be imposed on us; we must either undertake the task ourselves or, at the very least, accede to the divine solicitation to aid in the formation of our character. Yet the capacity to cooperate presupposes the ability to be uncooperative, and if our cooperation is important, a person can also choose not to cooperate and forever maintain this uncooperative stance. Furthermore, it is possible that there are no situations in which God could put the individual such that if that person were in that situation, that person would freely change his or her mind and cooperate with God. Hence, it is possible that some persons end up in hell whether any actually end up there or not; thus necessary universalism is false.

This argument is, I believe, telling against necessary universalism. The way I have put this argument, and the way I will continue to use the argument in the discussion that follows, assumes that persons have free will in a sense that denies that our choices are determined. Notice, however, that this free will position can be false and yet still undermine necessary universalism. All that is required is that the free will position is *possibly* true, for necessary universalism claims that in no possible world could any person end up in hell. So, although I discuss this matter under the supposition that persons actually are free in the relevant sense, all the argument requires is the possible truth of the doctrine of free will.

Although I have claimed that the free will argument is telling against necessary universalism, defenders of that position have not always found the argument convincing. They have developed responses to it that we must consider, if we are to give the position of necessary universalism a fair hearing. As far as I know, a necessary universalist might respond to this argument in only three ways. One way is to argue God would not—indeed, could not—create free beings who would ultimately reject him; if he creates any free beings at all, he could create only those who would not choose separation from him. This response focuses on the nature of God. The other two responses focus elsewhere. The first of these downplays the importance of human freedom, claiming instead that freedom should be overridden in some cases in order to gain more important moral goods or avoid important moral evils. The final response denies that anyone could freely reject God forever. On the face of it, this last line seems perhaps the least promising, but Thomas Talbott has defended both it and the relative unimportance of human freedom.[19] According to Talbott, it is not possible for persons to choose to damn themselves, and even if it were possible, God should override human freedom in such a case. He backs these claims with two arguments and his arguments are the most forceful presentations of these views I have found. I will examine these arguments first and later turn to the argument for the view that God could create only beings who would in the end choose salvation.

The Argument Against the Possibility of Choosing Damnation

Talbott says,

> The picture I get is something like this. Though a sinner, Belial, has learned, perhaps through bitter experience, that evil is always destructive, always contrary to his own interest as well as to the interest of others; and though he sees clearly that God is the ultimate source of all happiness and that disobedience can produce only greater and greater misery in his own life as well as in the life of others, Belial *freely* chooses eternal misery (or perhaps eternal oblivion) for himself nonetheless. The question that immediately arises here is: What could possible qualify as a motive for such a choice? As long as any ignorance, or deception, or bondage to desire remains, it is open to God to transform a sinner without interfering with human freedom; but once all ignorance and deception and bondage to desire is removed, so that a person is truly "free" to choose, there can no longer by any motive for choosing eternal misery for oneself.[20]

This argument is in the form of a dilemma concerning how a person might end up choosing damnation. Either such a choice is subject to interfering factors or it is not. To the extent that a person's choice is affected by "interfering" factors such as ignorance, deception, and the like, God can eliminate this interference without affecting the freedom of the person to choose. If God eliminates all interference, however, the person would no longer have a motive for choosing damnation and hence would not choose it. On either horn of the dilemma, no possibility exists for a person to choose damnation.

Talbott's argument recognizes that the internal features leading to action are both cognitive and affective. He first assumes that no cognitive mistake has been made in determining whether to choose hell and then questions what possible motive could lead to such a choice. Both parts of his argument have problems. First, Talbott assumes that God can remove any ignorance or mistaken belief on the cognitive side that leads a person to regrettable choices. In particular, God corrects the mistaken impression that self-interested choices lead to happiness. This view of the relationship between cognition and the will is controversial. Most important, it may be incompatible with the lessons to be learned from the way in which our complete view of the world confronts experience in a holistic fashion. Epistemologists and philosophers of science have come to realize that experience might teach us that our complete picture of the world is mistaken, but it cannot always teach us precisely where it is mistaken. A simple scientific example illustrates this point. Suppose a scientist accepts a Newtonian theory N and uses it, together with some understanding of initial conditions, to deduce the orbital pattern of planet P. This scientist then tests the theory by observation and notes that the orbital pattern varies quite significantly from the predicted pattern. Experience has indicated that the scientist's views are incorrect, but experience cannot tell him whether theory N is mistaken or the understanding of the initial conditions is mistaken (he might, for example, introduce an auxiliary hypothesis that the perturbations in the orbital pattern are due to the gravitational attraction of a hitherto undiscovered planet P'). Equally significant, the scientist might refuse to grant the truth of the observation statement. Presumably, he cannot deny that the observation statement seems to be true, but he might deny that it really is true. He might, by some extraordinary feat of obstinacy and irrationality (from our perspective at least), maintain theory N plus his understanding of the initial conditions by dismissing all contrary experiences as illusory. On a more global scale, this same phenomenon might happen with complete pictures of the world or approaches to life. A person might succeed in dismissing any attempt to be taught that one's picture of the world is mistaken by interpreting contrary experiences as illusory or by concluding that these contrary experiences call for the introduction of further auxiliary hypotheses. As a little reflection shows, there is no limit to the possibilities that might be employed to save a view of the world, and no way to guarantee what people will learn by introducing them to experiential anomalies for their view. Most important in the present context is that this pattern of response to experience, however irrational we might care to characterize it, might be a willful response of an individual to experience. Perhaps willfulness is beyond the pale of possibility in simple, ordinary cases of belief formation and sustenance (for example, I do not choose now to believe that there is a computer screen in front of me; it is not somehow directly "up to me" whether I believe this claim); yet, when we come to more global issues, such as the refusal to allow experience to count against a view of the world or certain parts of it, there surely is a possibility that such a response pattern is something I choose and for which I am responsible. So it is not clear that Talbott is entitled to the assumption that God can remove any source of ignorance without disturbing the freedom of the individual.

When we put aside worries about the cognitive side and focus instead on the affective dimension, things do not get much better. In order for Talbott's argument to be capable of rescuing necessary universalism, two claims must be true. The first is that if no motive for choosing damnation exists, a person cannot choose damnation; the second claim is that if all interfering factors are eliminated, a person can have no motive for choosing a bad alternative. These two claims involve the difficult and interrelated notions of an interfering factor, a motive, and free choice. In order to evaluate Talbott's argument, we need a clear understanding of these notions, and we can begin to understand them by considering a case of proper behavior that is freely chosen—say, freely giving money to a charitable cause. Presumably, even such behavior is motivated in some way or other (perhaps the child of a friend has leukemia, and one is giving to the leukemia society in response to one's feelings for the child and the friend), so freedom does not require the absence of motives. Freedom does, however, require the absence of interfering factors, at least interfering factors of a certain kind. First, external interference can be incompatible with true freedom; for example, a person is not freely sitting in a chair when the sole reason for being in the chair is that he or she is tied to it. More important in the present context is the role that certain kinds of internal interference play in determining whether and to what extent an action is truly free. Internal interfering factors are certainly possible; for example, wicked brain surgeons might implant devices in one's brain that cause abnormal hormonal production that might lead to excessive behavior of a certain sort. Clearly, such action is not completely free because it is partially the product of an internal interfering factor. Talbott cites three examples of what he wishes to count as internal interfering factors: ignorance, deception, and bondage to desire. The first two are cognitive in nature, and we have discussed these features. That leaves only the last of the three, and the question we must ask concerns the relation between it and freedom: Is freedom affected by the removal of bondage to desire?

Note that Talbott's phrasing includes the locution bondage to', for it would be a mistake to think that desires and other affective states in themselves interfere with freedom. This mistake is serious enough that we must disabuse ourselves of it before proceeding. If freedom were incompatible with desires and other affective states, the only persons who could be truly free would be those without desires or interests of any sort. Nothing that engages in action of any sort could be like that, for the nature of action is bound up with having intentions, goals, and plans, and being characterized by other affective states. If absence of desire were important for freedom, then in order for the blessed in heaven to be truly free, they would have to fail to love God with their whole hearts, souls, minds, and strength; they would have to fail to desire to be with God forever; and they would have to fail to admire and adore and be thankful to God for what he has done for them. Hence, it is crucial that Talbott conceive of the interfering factor as involving a kind of bondage to an affective state, for affective states themselves are critical to the very notion of agency. At best, only when an affective state "imprisons" us could it damage our freedom, and that is why the language of bondage is so crucial to Talbott's point.

When having a certain desire amounts to being in bondage to it is difficult to determine. We do not need to decide this issue, however, to reach a conclusion regarding Talbott's claims. To sustain necessary universalism, anytime one has a desire for something evil, acting on that desire must involve being in bondage to desire. To see that a defense of necessary universalism in the face of the free will argument requires the truth of this claim, suppose it is false. If it is false, then in at least one case the desire for evil will still be present when all interfering factors are removed. But if this desire is present, there will be no reason that a person could not choose to view the satisfaction of this desire as more important than presence with God, and hence choose evil over and against union with God. Hence, in order for Talbott's argument to rescue necessary universalism, any action based on a desire for something evil must imply bondage to the desire in question.

This claim, however, is obviously false; one can be motivated to choose evil and yet the actions that result from these motivations be fully free. One way for this to occur is for a person to will that a desire for evil not be extinguished and that it affect future actions. It remains a possibility that some persons have a fundamental, basic desire and intention to pursue evil over good, perhaps by preferring self-exaltation or self-determination over anything else; such persons, we might say, are fundamentally depraved. God could remove the impact of developed habits and the like that result from the depravity, but removing the depravity itself simply amounts to overriding the will rather than freeing it. The only way to remove fundamental depravity without overriding the will is for a person to give up his or her claims on self-determination and ask for divine intervention—in a word, to undergo complete conversion.

It is therefore false that any nonideal motivation constitutes a factor that interferes with a person's freedom. Hence, even though

God can eliminate interfering factors, doing so provides no guarantee that a person will thereby come to choose the good. Moreover,
such a guarantee is just what necessary universalism requires, and
hence this attempt to rescue necessary universalism from the free
will argument fails. Remove all the interfering factors, and some
persons might still desire anything over union with God and thus
choose damnation because anything is preferable, in their minds, to
the abandonment of self that union with God implies.

The Argument Against the Overriding Importance of Freedom

Talbott has yet another argument that might be marshaled here on
behalf of necessary universalism. He claims that if the idea of a
rational agent freely choosing damnation is assumed to be coherent,
God should override the freedom of any individual who makes such
a choice.

> [E]verlasting separation is the kind of evil that a loving God would
> prevent even if it meant interfering with human freedom in certain
> ways. Consider the two kinds of conditions under which we human
> beings feel justified in interfering with the freedom of others. We feel
> justified, first of all, in preventing one person from doing irreparable
> harm, or what may appear to us as irreparable harm, to another.
> . . . We also feel justified in preventing others from doing irreparable
> harm to themselves; a loving father may . . . physically overpower
> his daughter in an effort to prevent her from committing sui-
> cide. . . . So . . . a loving God . . . could never permit one person
> to destroy the very possibility of future happiness in another;
> and . . . he could never permit his loved ones to destroy the very
> possibility of future happiness in themselves.[21]

Talbott argues that we can interfere with the freedom of others to
prevent both harm to others and harm to the one doing the action.
He concludes from these points that God could never allow anyone
to make a choice that precludes the very possibility of future happiness. Although he never explicitly states the claim, clearly Talbott
thinks of this last description as a description of hell: Being in hell
precludes the very possibility of achieving future happiness.

There are two mistakes in this argument. The first concerns
Talbott's account of justified intervention in cases of suicide; the
second is that the conclusion that needs to be drawn—that God
would interfere in a person's freedom to prevent one from ending up
in hell—does not follow. I defend each of these claims in turn.

Talbott's account of the justification for interfering to prevent a
murder is correct, for we are justified in infringing on the freedom of

some to prevent harm to others. Talbott has not, however, correctly analyzed the case of suicide. Sometimes interference in cases of suicide is justified, but it is not justified solely because suicide causes irreparable harm. We can interfere when a person is subject to a temporary depression; in such a case, what justifies the interference is the likelihood that things will change or the likelihood that, under the duress of depression, the person is not making a decision she would make in less difficult conditions. We can interfere when a person underestimates his prospects for the future; again, a justification similar to the last sort is available, for when the person comes to see things more clearly, he will agree that we should have intervened. We can also interfere medically when some treatable physiological condition interferes with a person's judgment in such a way that the person is suicidal because of the way the sickness interferes with the rationality of the individual in question. We can also intervene when a person does not really know quite what she is doing, as is the case when dealing with adolescents or small children, for example. None of these justifications, however, appeals only to the purely objective fact that harm is being done. Rather, what justifies our intervention is the fact that the person will come, or will likely come, to see that his choice of death was not what he really wanted or would have wanted if he had reflected carefully. Alternatively, if we are fully convinced and it is true that the person is competent to choose, is rational in choosing suicide, and cannot be persuaded otherwise, then, from a purely moral point of view, interference is not justified (except insofar as the suicide has consequences for other persons such as dependent children).

Some qualifications are in order so that the point is not obscured by unrelated matters. From social and political points of view, interference in cases of suicide may be encouraged regardless of the mental state of the person in question because of the social utility in such a practice. We would do well, however, to distinguish social and political obligations and duties from purely moral ones. Another point is that the least risky approach to suicide, given our frail abilities to read others' minds, might be intervention. We perhaps should intervene because we are fallible and failure to intervene may not be remediable. Still, these issues do not touch on the purely moral point made previously, that objective harm is not the crucial moral element in determining whether intervention is justified. The point might be put as follows: If we were omniscient, able to read the minds of others and predict the future infallibly, the crucial question we should ask in deciding whether to intervene in a possible suicide concerns what the person chooses and would continue to choose.

This crucial factor, as noted before, is a *defeasible* one; that is, it can be overridden by other moral concerns, such as the welfare of the children of the individual. It can also be overridden by the choice being subjectively irrational (irrational by the lights of the individual in question) or by the likelihood that the choice will become subjectively irrational in the future.[22] In addition, there are difficult epistemic concerns to be addressed concerning how sure we need to be that a person would continue (rationally) to choose suicide, for in this life at least there is usually a possibility that things will get better or that a person will come to view the actual circumstances in a more favorable light. However, these features are relevant only to individuals with limited intellects and as such cannot be used to draw a conclusion about when a violation of freedom by God would be morally warranted. Instead, a proper understanding of the moral dimensions of suicide reveals an important dimension of inviolability of moral freedom. Contrary to what Talbott claims, freedom is sometimes more important than the harm that might result from an exercise of freedom. Hence the fact that sometimes freedom can be infringed upon legitimately does not show that God should infringe upon the freedom of any person headed for hell.

A further point to note in the context of heaven and hell is that if one overriding of the will is to occur in this fashion to prevent the choice of separation from God, a whole host of similar violations of freedom will have to occur as well. Presumably the person's will cannot be let loose; he is depraved and would choose separation again. God could do something like metaphysically lobotomizing the patient to secure a kind of dull acquiescence for all eternity (although it is hard to see how this would fit with having in heaven those who love God with their whole "heart, mind, soul, and strength").[23] Obviously such an action would not be for the purpose of securing the highest and best for such individuals. In fact, no matter what God does to secure the presence of a wholly rebellious individual in heaven, we will have a paradigm case of treating a person as a mere means to another's ends. There is, then, good reason to think that reflecting about justified intervention in cases of suicide does not generate adequate grounds for thinking that God should override the wills of the wholly rebellious to secure their presence in heaven.

My argument that God should not always override the freedom of rebellious individuals to secure their presence in heaven depends on the assumption that God foreknows what free individuals will want, desire, and choose in the future. I argued that intervention could be justified in cases of suicide on the pragmatic grounds of our own fallibility; we might be justified in stopping a suicide because failure to act is irremediable, and we might not know for sure that a person will never conceive his or her situation to have gotten better. If God cannot foreknow what free individuals will want, desire and choose in the future, then he is no better off than we with respect to these pragmatic considerations. We might wonder, then, whether Talbott could find a justification for necessary universalism by denying the possibility of foreknowledge of the required sort and by appealing to the pragmatics of the situation.

Because Talbott's argument depends on an analogy between suicide cases and the case of consignment to hell, for it to support necessary universalism, it must show that our inability to know the future always and necessarily justifies interference in cases of suicide, and the truth of this claim is simply not clear. Some cases, such as suicide in the face of the unending and excruciating pain of terminal illness, may be clear enough that we have no right to interfere. This fact is important in the present context because this might just be the way a wholly rebellious will conceives and experiences the presence of God, distorted though it may be. So even without the assumption of God's infallible knowledge of the future, considerations concerning justified intervention to prevent suicide do not relieve necessary universalism of the difficulty posed by the free will argument.

I noted earlier two mistakes in Talbott's argument, the first having to do with a misrepresentation of how intervention can be justified in cases of suicide and the second being that the conclusion Talbott draws from his claims about justified intervention is a non sequitur. Having discussed the first point, we turn here to the second. Recall that the conclusion Talbott draws in the quote at the beginning of this subsection is that God could never allow anyone to make a choice that precludes the very possibility of future happiness. Given the context of the article, clearly Talbott thinks of this last description as a description of hell: Being in hell precludes the very possibility of achieving future happiness. Why conceive of hell in this way? Recall that one of the problems discussed for contingent universalism is the way defenses of it piggyback off defects of the strong view of hell. Universalists typically commit the fallacy of false dilemma by pointing out that hell on the strong view is so bad that universalism would have to be true. The conclusion Talbott draws appears to be just another instance of that same strategy. One begins by identifying hell in terms of the strong view, and then one argues that sending anyone to a hell of this sort is so irremediably bad that universalism must be true. The mistake here is just that of false dilemma arguments. If the strong view is morally objectionable—if there really is a problem of hell—then one cannot piggyback one's favored view of hell on the inadequacies of the strong view. Too many other possibilities need to be considered.

We can summarize as follows the points I have been making about justified intervention in cases of suicide and its relationship to the doctrine of hell. First, Talbott is wrong in thinking that objective harm is the right criterion to appeal to in cases of suicide. At least as important is the person's subjective conception of the situation. Also important is the subjective rationality of this conception, and the likelihood that this conception is permanent. This last consideration may justify intervention on the pragmatic ground that we cannot be sure enough that the conception in question is permanent. Two remarks are in order about this pragmatic justification of intervention: It is irrelevant to an omniscient being who knows the future infallibly; it is far from clear that such a pragmatic justification would license interference in every case of attempted suicide. As noted before, some cases, such as suicide in the face of the unending and excruciating pain of terminal illness, may be clear enough that interference is unwarranted. This fact is important in the present context because this might just be the experience of the wholly rebellious will in the presence of God: Such an individual may conceive and experience eternal intimacy with God as unendingly and excruciatingly painful. The most important point, however, is the lack of connection between considerations of suicide and the conclusion Talbott wishes to draw—that God could not send anyone to hell—which follows only when one first accepts the No Escape Thesis of the strong view of hell. This pattern of argument is guilty of a false dilemma. If the No Escape Thesis is so problematic that one can preserve it only by accepting necessary universalism, there are still two ways to remedy this situation. Talbott assumes that the remedy is to accept necessary universalism, even at the expense of honoring freedom, but as we have seen, his arguments against the overriding importance of freedom fail to establish this conclusion. More important, even if he could establish that freedom should be overridden in some cases, he would not have shown that necessary universalism is true. His discussion assumes the truth of the No Escape Thesis, and his perception that the impossibility of leaving hell is irremediably bad drives the discussion. Yet, if the No Escape Thesis drives the discussion, developing an account of hell that begins from a denial of this thesis would be appropriate. The proper conclusion to draw in ending this section, then, is that Talbott's arguments against the overriding importance of human freedom fail to rescue necessary universalism from the free will argument against it.

God's Nature and the Choice of Hell

The last attempt to salvage necessary universalism from the threat posed to it by the free will argument supposes that one could explain the impossibility of a person's ultimately rejecting God by appeal to what God would or would not have created in the first place. The claim involved is that if God in his omniscience foresees that certain people would reject him eternally, his love could not allow the creation of beings who will not realize their potential in relationship with him. God's loving character metaphysically bars the creation of any such being. Hence, no being could possibly end up in hell.

The first point to note is that this argument does not constitute a defense of necessary universalism. This position grants the possibility of someone ending up in hell, and if this possibility is granted, necessary universalism must be rejected, even if in fact no world God could create could be such a world. At most, what might be true is a cousin view of necessary universalism, according to which there could be no world created by God in which someone ends up in hell.

Nonetheless, the related view is of interest enough that we ought to consider whether it can be maintained. Let us call this view "creatable universalism," for according to it, any possibility of an individual ending up in hell involves an uncreatable individual. So no creatable individual might end up in hell. On this view, there are possibilities that God could not create; in fact, maintaining that there are possibilities God could not create is essential to the credibility of creatable universalism. If God could actualize or create any possibility, then creatable universalism would collapse into necessary universalism and be subject to the free will objection. So some argument is needed for thinking that some possibilities could not be actualized or created by God.

We can approach this same point from a different perspective. In describing the motivations for the response to the free will argument, it is easy to slip between the language of 'could' and 'would': we can easily slip, that is, from the claim that God *would not* create any being who would reject him to the claim that God *could not* create such a person. The first of these claims is of no use here, for it

is compatible with the existence of creatable free beings who ultimately reject God. Hence, it can only establish the truth of contingent universalism, and we have already seen the inadequacy of that
position in solving the problem of hell. So what is needed here is the
strongest modal language, the language of impossibility. What must
be defended is that God *could not*—not merely that he *would not*—
create any individual who would ultimately reject him. What results
is a hybrid universalist position. It is a version of contingent universalism, because it grants the logical possibility that a person end up
in hell. Yet it also maintains a type of necessity to the fact that no
one will end up in hell because it is logically impossible for God to
create such an individual. Perhaps in such a hybrid position can be
found a route to escape the force of the objections to both necessary
and contingent universalism.

It is difficult to see what sort of argument could be used to
establish the strong modal claim that God could not create anyone
who would choose hell, but an argument given by Alvin Plantinga
for the claim that there are possible worlds God could not create
might be of some use.[24] If there are worlds God could not create,
then perhaps a subclass of these worlds are all the worlds in which
free individuals choose hell. This is the only argument (of which I
am aware) that might be used to support the position of creatable
universalism, so we can reach a decision about its plausibility by
determining whether Plantinga's argument is successful. His argument is set in the context of an example about Curley, where the
question is whether Curley would freely accept a $20,000 bribe if it
were offered to him. Plantinga's summary of the argument for the
existence of worlds God cannot actualize is as follows:

> Was it within God's power, supposing him omnipotent, to actualize
> just any possible world that includes his existence? No. In a nutshell,
> the reason is this. There is a possible world W where God strongly
> actualizes a totality T of states of affairs including Curley's being free
> with respect to taking the bribe, and where Curley takes the bribe. But
> there is another possible world W^* where God actualizes the very
> same states of affairs and where Curley rejects the bribe. Now suppose
> it is true as a matter of fact that if God had actualized T, Curley would
> have accepted the bribe: then God could not have actualized W^*. And
> if, on the other hand, Curley would have rejected the bribe, had God
> actualized T, then God could not have actualized W. So either way
> there are worlds God could not have actualized.[25]

Plantinga argues that if it is true that Curley would accept the bribe
if offered, then God cannot actualize the possible world in which
Curley would reject the bribe if offered. Hence, according to Plan-

tinga, Leibniz was wrong: There are possible worlds God could not actualize.

Before embarking on substantive criticism of this argument, note some asides. The first concerns Plantinga's appeal to counterfactuals about what would be freely done in certain circumstances. Some discussion of these counterfactuals assumes the Law of Conditional Excluded Middle (LCEM) for counterfactuals, according to which for any propositions p and q, either p counterfactually implies q or it implies $\sim q$. This argument presupposes LCEM in contrast to the prevailing opinion.[26] Later on, however, Plantinga abandons this assumption,[27] so in the present discussion, I ignore the fact that the argument presupposes LCEM. The second aside concerns a mistake in the previous quoted passage concerning the logic of counterfactuals. The passage begins with a counterfactual having as antecedent that Curley is offered a bribe and then moves from this counterfactual to one with a strengthened antecedent, involving a "totality of states of affairs including Curley's being free with respect to taking the bribe." Plantinga's discussion assumes that the counterfactual with the strengthened antecedent has the same truth value as the original counterfactual. It need not, however, for the logic of counterfactuals is known not to permit strengthening of antecedents.[28] Nevertheless, I see no reason to think that the truth of Plantinga's position is undermined by this point, so I will ignore it in what follows. Third, this discussion is closely tied to a position Plantinga holds known as Molinism, according to which God's knowledge of counterfactuals of freedom—counterfactuals of the form *If S were to be put in circumstances C and were free with respect to doing A, S would do A*—is prevolitional knowledge, that is, knowledge of truths that are true independent of the exercise of God's will. Plantinga's argument assumes the truth of Molinism, so if Molinism is false, Plantinga's argument will have to be abandoned. I shall not be arguing in this way, for I share Plantinga's view on this matter. A remark about Molinism might be helpful, however, in that thinking that one can infer Plantinga's anti-Leibnizian conclusion from Molinist premises alone may be tempting. Such an argument would infer that Leibniz lapsed in thinking that God could create any possible world by arguing as follows: "If there is something A God could do to make p false, and God did not do A, then God's choosing not to do A is responsible for p's being true, in which case God's knowledge of p is not prevolitional; hence, if Molinism is true, there is nothing God could do to make any false counterfactual of freedom true, and hence nothing God could do to actualize a world in which are true both the antecedent and consequent of a false counterfactual of freedom." This Molinist argument should be rejected, however, for if a non-deterministic conception of human freedom is even just possibly true, this argument is unsound. Suppose I am freely working on this paper and that God knows this truth. Clearly, God's knowledge here is not based directly on his will; that is, it is prevolitional, for the contrary assumption denies the freedom of the action, in the relevant sense of 'freedom'.[29] Could God do something to make the claim in question false? Surely he could. Does it follow from this last fact that God's choosing not to make the claim false makes it true? Clearly not, for by hypothesis the action is free and hence not made true by anyone other than me. So it does not follow from the claim that God knows p prevolitionally that God could not make p false. It only follows that he did not exercise his will so as to make it true. Hence Molinism as such, with its emphasis on God's prevolitional knowledge of counterfactuals of freedom, does not support the anti-Leibnizian position Plantinga takes that there are some possibilities God cannot actualize. If Leibniz is wrong for Plantinga-like reasons, the reasons must have to do with the nature of counterfactuals of freedom themselves, rather than grounds relating to the character of God's knowledge of them. That is precisely what Plantinga's previously quoted argument attempts to show. Unfortunately, that argument fails.

The fundamental problem is that Plantinga's argument rests on an unduly restrictive conception of what it takes for God to have been able to actualize a world. If Curley would accept the bribe if offered, Plantinga thinks God could have actualized W, the world in which Curley is offered the bribe and freely accepts. Let us call the counterfactual about Curley a "counterfactual of freedom," and a world W in which both antecedent and consequent of this counterfactual of freedom are true "a world corresponding to the counterfactual of freedom." Plantinga thinks God cannot create or actualize any world corresponding to false counterfactuals of freedom. This conception, however, is too restrictive, for what counterfactuals are true depends on which world is actual. Counterfactuals true relative to the actual world might have been false if some other world were actual. Suppose, for example, that W is the actual world, so that it is true that if Curley were offered the bribe he would accept it. This claim is compatible with the claim that if some other world (W*) were actual, then the counterfactual "if Curley were offered the bribe, he would freely reject it" would have been true. Furthermore, no reason has been given for denying that W* is actualizable; yet, if it is actualizable, then there is every reason to think that the state of affairs of Curley's being offered the bribe and freely rejecting it is also actualizable. This state of affairs could have been actualized by God, had he actualized W^* instead of W. This point suggests that a broader construal is appropriate of what worlds are actualizable; that is, a world is actualizable if it is actualizable from any world that is actualizable on Plantinga's more restrictive conception. If God could have done something so that W^* would have been actual, then God could have actualized a world (call it W^{**}) in which Curley is offered the bribe and rejects it, even though it is actually true that if Curley were offered the bribe he would accept it. To put the point metaphorically, W^{**} should count as actualizable if there is a "route" through the domain of possible worlds that God could have taken (by actualizing states of affairs that moved him from one world in the sequence to the next) such that, if he had, the counterfactual of freedom to which W^{**} corresponds would have been true, that is, W^* would have been actual. Plantinga's conception restricts considerably the routes allowed for a world to count as actualizable. If we continue to suppose that Curley would accept the bribe if offered, that shows that there is no direct (i.e., one-step) route from the actual world to W^{**}, the world in which Curley is offered the bribe and rejects it, and Plantinga concludes from this that W^{**} is not actualizable, which is a mistake. As long as God can do something to "get to" W^*, the world in which Curley would reject the bribe if offered, from some world that has already been granted to be actualizable, then W^{**} itself is actualizable (although the route involves more than one step). That is, if we have a class of worlds X that are assumed to be actualizable, then if W^{**} is a world corresponding to counterfactual of freedom C, where C is true in some member of X, then W^{**} is actualizable by God. So if there is an actually true counterfactual of the form "if God were to actualize A, then W^* would have been actual," then, even though it is actually false that if Curley were offered the bribe, he would have rejected it, it is nonetheless true that W^{**} (the world where Curley is offered the bribe and rejects it) might have been actualized by God. For if God had actualized A, W^* would have been actual, and from the perspective of W^*, W^{**} is actualizable, because in W^* Curley would have rejected the bribe if offered. So even though there is no one-step route through the realm of worlds to W^{**}, there still might be a multiple-step route to it through some member of the class X of worlds that can be actualized in one step relative to the actual world.

The difference between this conception and Plantinga's conception can now be put succinctly, employing the relativistic notion of one world's being actualizable relative to another world. On my account, we define the notion of actualizability *simpliciter* in terms of one world's being actualizable relative to another world. My claim is that a world is actualizable *simpliciter* if it is actualizable relative to any other actualizable world, that is, if it corresponds to a counterfactual of freedom that is true in some world that is actualizable relative to the actual world. And what is it for a world to be actualizable relative to the actual world? It is for that world to be a world in which both the antecedent and consequent are true of some counterfactual that is true in the actual world and is such that God can make the antecedent true. So, whereas Plantinga's account restricts what worlds are actualizable to those actualizable relative to the actual world, this broader understanding of actualizability allows that worlds are actualizable even when they fail to be actualizable relative to the actual world. My argument is that we have no good reason to maintain the more restrictive conception. If God can "get to" a world in some fashion or other, that should be enough to say that the world is creatable. It should not matter whether God can get there in one step.

Given the possibility and intuitive appeal of this broader understanding of which worlds are actualizable (*simpliciter*), Plantinga's argument fails to establish that W^{**} (the world in which Curley is offered the bribe and rejects it) is unactualizable even if we assume that Curley would accept the bribe if offered. All Plantinga's argument shows is that W^{**} is unactualizable relative to the actual world. In order to show that W^{**} is unactualizable *simpliciter*, Plantinga needs to show more: that there is no actualizable world relative to which W^{**} is actualizable.

My argument against Plantinga's claims begins from a set of worlds assumed to be actualizable and then enlarges the set by adding any worlds actualizable relative to the initial members. One might wonder whether this argument succeeds only if I assume that the initial set of actualizable worlds has more than one member in it (obviously, the actual world is actualizable, so the initial set must at least include that world). One need not worry here, however, for even if the initial set of actualizable worlds is limited to the actual world, Plantinga's argument fails. We can think of the class of actualizable worlds as a hierarchy of levels where world x is a member of level n (greater than or equal to 1) if and only if there is some world y at level $n-1$ such that x is actualizable relative to y. Even if the base level of this construction includes only the actual world, it does not follow that W^* is unactualizable, which could follow only if this construction were limited to two levels, so that the only actualizable worlds were worlds actualizable relative to the actual world. Clearly, however, the hierarchy need not have only two levels, so Plantinga's argument fails even if we assume that the initial set of actualizable worlds includes only one member, namely, the actual world.

In the passage containing Plantinga's argument that I quoted earlier, note that Plantinga does not focus on the counterfactual *If Curley were offered the bribe, he would accept it.* Instead, he focuses on a counterfactual with a stronger antecedent that Plantinga calls "*T*," one including Curley's being free with respect to his accepting the bribe, but also including "every state of affairs God strongly actualizes in *W.*"[30] This difference, however, is inessential, for my objection that the hierarchy of actualization includes more than two levels is not affected by whether we are examining counterfactuals with restricted antecedents or more global antecedents such as *T*. It still might be that if God had actualized global antecedent $T' \neq T$, then if he had actualized *T*, Curley would have rejected the bribe, even though, as things actually stand, God's strongly actualizing *T* counterfactually implies Curley's accepting the bribe.

This response also shows why another objection to my argument can be rejected. By assuming the rule of importation for counterfactuals, one might respond on behalf of Plantinga in two ways. First, my account of actualizability could be said to collapse into Plantinga's account because, by importation, $\ulcorner p \rightarrow (A \rightarrow B) \urcorner$ is equivalent to $\ulcorner (p \& A) \rightarrow B \urcorner$. One might then go on to point out that, because the antecedents of the conditionals Plantinga considers are already maximal, nothing could be added to them except that which engenders a contradiction; and, of course, God cannot be held responsible for bringing about any world that would have resulted from his strongly actualizing a contradictory state of affairs.

This entire line of thinking is mistaken, however, for the rule of importation is not valid on counterfactuals. Consider the pair of counterfactuals *If Nixon had not resigned, then it would have been true that if he had resigned, he would no longer have been president* and *If Nixon had not resigned, then it would have been true that if he had resigned, he still would have remained president.* Inspection reveals that the first of these claims is obviously true and the second is obviously false. Furthermore, even if this assessment of the truth values of these claims is mistaken, reflection on the semantic treatment of these claims shows that it is quite easy for counterfac-

tuals such as these to diverge in truth value. On the standard semantics, we are instructed first to consider close worlds where Nixon
does not resign. Then, from the vantage point of such worlds, we are
instructed to see if there is a closest world in which Nixon does
resign. If there is, then the truth value of the two claims is determined by whether that world is also a world in which Nixon remains
president.

If importation were an acceptable rule for counterfactuals, this
way of approaching the truth value of these sentences would be
mistaken. The semantical treatment of counterfactuals with necessarily false antecedents is simple: They are all trivially true. Yet, on
the semantical tale here, the existence of closest worlds of the sort
described yields that one of the counterfactuals is true and the other
false. If importation were acceptable, both claims would be trivially
true and necessarily so. So no objection to my argument against
Plantinga or my alternative conception of actualizability can succeed if it relies on the rule of importation.

One might also think that my objection to Plantinga's argument
rests too centrally on the standard semantics for counterfactuals, for
I have appealed to the device of possible worlds in arguing for a
broader construal of actualizability *simpliciter*. It is true that I have
resorted to the language of possible worlds to make my point, but
that language is not essential, for the same point can be made purely
in syntactic terms. Even if it is false that Curley would reject the
bribe if offered, it is still possible that there is some contingent
proposition p such that (1) God could make it true, and (2), if it were
true, it would be true that Curley would reject the bribe if offered.
More generally, suppose that $\ulcorner A \twoheadrightarrow B \urcorner$ is false. Still, there might be
some other proposition p such that the counterfactual $\ulcorner p \twoheadrightarrow (A \twoheadrightarrow B) \urcorner$
is true. That is, there may be some proposition such that if it were
true, then $\ulcorner A \twoheadrightarrow B \urcorner$ would be true. If so, however, God could actualize
the truth of $\ulcorner A \twoheadrightarrow B \urcorner$ by actualizing the truth of p; and if he can
actualize the truth of $\ulcorner A \twoheadrightarrow B \urcorner$ he can actualize the truth of $A \& B$ and,
therefore, to resort to worlds-talk again, an $A \& B$-world. He could not
do it in one step, for that would require that $\ulcorner A \twoheadrightarrow B \urcorner$ is true. He can,
however, do it in two steps: First make p true, and then some world
where both A and B are true will be actualizable in one step.

This argument can be generalized further. Even if there should
be no value for p of the sort required, there still might be some finite
set of ordered propositions $p_1 \ldots p_n$ relative to the false proposi-
tion $\ulcorner A \twoheadrightarrow B \urcorner$ such that for some $1 \leq m < n$, $A \twoheadrightarrow B = p_n$ and some
claim of the form $\ulcorner p_1 \twoheadrightarrow [\ldots p_1 \ldots \twoheadrightarrow (p_m \twoheadrightarrow \ldots \twoheadrightarrow p_n)] \urcorner$ is

true. That is, all that needs to be the case is that there is a finite string of propositions connected by counterfactual arrows to $\ulcorner A \rightarrow B \urcorner$ such that the parenthetical groupings begin with the rightmost connectives and work back to the leftmost, so the first counterfactual arrow connects p_1 with everything after it, and similarly for each p_i. If there is such a set of propositions, then God could actualize the world in which Curley rejects the bribe when offered. To do that, he would first have to actualize a world corresponding to the previous counterfactual, from the perspective of which a world corresponding to the first embedded counterfactual could be actualized directly, so that if he had actualized that world, then a world corresponding to the second embedded counterfactual could be actualized directly, and so on. We might then define different levels of actualizability as follows: Where $\ulcorner A \rightarrow B \urcorner$ is true, a world W^* where both A and B are true is actualizable$_0$. Where $n = 2$ in $p_1 \ldots p_n$, W^* is actualizable$_1$; and generally, W^* is actualizable$_{n-1}$ relative to the ordered set of propositions $p_1 \ldots p_n$. Note that this syntactic machinery, independently of any appeal to the semantics for counterfactuals, shows that Plantinga's argument should be rejected. Plantinga argues that some possible worlds cannot be created by God because they are not actualizable$_0$. This reason is insufficient. To sustain his charge that Leibniz lapsed, Plantinga needs to show that there are some possible worlds that, for any i, are not actualizable$_i$. So regardless of whether there are decisive reasons to be dissatisfied with the Lewis-Stalnaker semantics for counterfactuals, there still are good reasons for rejecting Plantinga's argument.

Given the failure of this argument, we have no reason to suppose that creatable universalism is a distinct position from necessary universalism. Because of this fact, no difficulties facing neccessary universalism can be assuaged by substituting for it creatable universalism. If either position is to be maintained against the free will objection, it must reply to that objection either by arguing that free will ought to be overridden if a person were to choose hell or by arguing that it is impossible to choose damnation. As we have seen, however, neither of these alternatives provides an adequate defense of necessary universalism against the free will objection. I conclude, then, that necessary universalism does not offer a solution to the problem of hell. Necessary universalism may offer a comforting response to the question of why God would create anyone who chooses hell, but it is a comfort bought at the price of verisimilitude.

On Abandoning the Retribution Thesis

The final simple alternative to the strong view of hell denies (H4), the Retribution Thesis. There are two quite different ways to deny (H4). The most obvious is to deny that the purpose of hell is retributive in nature. A more subtle denial of (H4) retains the retributive character of hell but denies that it is retribution for one's earthly life and character that justifies hell. Instead, it is the combination of one's earthly life plus the time between death and the final consummation that retributively demands hell for certain individuals. We saw this view earlier when discussing second chance theories that deny the No Escape Thesis. It, too, is a second chance theory, but it does not deny the No Escape Thesis. Instead, it holds that consignment to hell occurs only at the final consummation of all things, and that one consigned to hell at that point has failed to make the right choices both prior to and after death. That is, one is given a second chance (or many chances) after death to meet the conditions required for entrance into heaven, and one's failure to meet these conditions both before and after death justifies consignment to hell.

Brian Hebblethwaite holds just such a view. He says, in commenting on the relationship between the particular judgment at death and the last judgment prior to the final consummation,

> Even in New Testament times, we find the idea that men and women are judged already by their own reaction to the incarnate Word that had come into their midst. There is no serious suggestion that such judgement here on earth is final and irrevocable at any time prior to death. . . . According to tradition, it is only at death that the set of a man's will is discerned irrevocably as bent on heaven or hell. . . . But if we question this idea of the finality of death and allow for further opportunities of repentance and growth beyond the grave, it follows that the judgement brought upon oneself by one's reaction to the love of God encountered after death is no more permanent and final than the judgement experienced throughout an earthly life. Only in the end, in the final consummation, does the creature's relation to God acquire a permanent, unchangeable character.[31]

Hebblethwaite believes that there is no finality to death in terms of heaven or hell. Instead, the judgment one experiences at death is qualitatively similar to the judgment one experiences on earth. Neither judgment is irrevocable; to the contrary, each such judgment leaves open the possibility of repentance and growth. There is, according to Hebblethwaite, a time at which this possibility of repentancè and growth is lost, however. At the final consummation, one's relation to God becomes permanent and unchangeable.

Conceived of as a simple alternative to the strong view of hell, this version of a second chance theory faces severe problems.[32] Like the strong view, it must explain what justifies the infinite punishment of hell imposed at the final consummation. The strong view is problematic because it fails to distinguish between different kinds of wrongs committed on earth and because of the severity of the punishment in relation to the offense, and this version of a second chance theory has no resources to solve these problems.

A general lesson can be learned here about second chance theories. Such theories hope to alleviate the weaknesses of the strong view by delaying the consequences of wrongdoing beyond the cutoff point maintained by the strong view. The purported solution to this moral difficulty is to give people another chance to avoid the consequences assigned for sin. If this second chance is refused, however, the problem does not disappear, for if a punishment is unduly harsh, it remains unduly harsh no matter how many chances a person is given to avoid it. The motivation for second chance doctrines thus quickly becomes transformed into a motivation for an infinite chance doctrine. Clearly, however, an infinite chance doctrine will not do. Any offering of another chance in this view involves a postponement of the consequences due to sin, and so if an infinite number of chances is required by justice, then the consequences at stake must be indefinitely postponed. Indefinitely postponed consequences, however, are no consequences at all. Thus the second chance doctrine degenerates quickly into the view that the problem of hell can be solved only by abandoning the doctrine altogether and maintaining instead that no consequences whatsoever are deserved by sin. That is the lesson to be learned: This kind of second chance view merely applies a superficial bandage to the cancer of the problem of hell. Insofar as it involves any way of avoiding the problem of hell, it can do so only by abandoning the doctrine entirely. As we saw earlier, however, abandoning the doctrine entirely does not solve the problem of hell.

If a simple alternative to the strong view is to be found that abandons the Retribution Thesis, it will have to do so by claiming that the justification for hell is not retributive in character. Richard Swinburne holds such a position:

> Now those who . . . resist a good desire will have such good desires again. But if they systematically resist desires of a certain kind, they

will gradually become the kind of person to whom such desires do not occur with any force. . . . A man who never resists his desires, trying to do the action which he perceives overall to be the best, gradually allows what he does to be determined entirely by the strength of his desires (as measured by the difficulty of resisting them). That is, he eliminates himself (as an agent doing the action of greatest perceived worth or allowing himself to be overcome by strong desire to do an action of lesser worth or simply choosing between actions of equal perceived worth). There is no longer a "he": the agent has turned into a mere theatre of conflicting desires of which the strongest automatically dictates "his" action. . . .

We may describe a man in this situation of having lost his capacity to overrule his desires as having "lost his soul." Such a man is a prisoner of bad desires. He can no longer choose to resist them by doing the action which he judges to be overall the best thing to do. He has no natural desires to do the actions of heaven and he cannot choose to do them because he sees them to be of supreme worth. There is no "he" left to make that choice.[33]

Swinburne holds that a person can act so that his desires for the good become extinguished and that, by so doing, a person eliminates his capacity of freedom and thereby eliminates even the barest possibility of reform.

If this position could be maintained, it would contribute significantly to solving the problems with the strong view of hell without much alteration in the general picture presented by that view. One of the problems for the strong view of hell is that it metes out immense punishment for seemingly minor offenses. On Swinburne's view, initial consignment in hell might be explained by a retributive model of punishment, but continued residence in hell would not be explained by that model. Integral to the retributive model is a determination of one's present condition on the basis of something that occurred in the time prior to the beginning of one's punishment. On Swinburne's view, one's continued presence in hell is not due to something that occurred in the earthly past but rather to the present condition of having lost one's soul. One's residence in hell is eternal, not because one has done something to deserve it, but rather because it is impossible for one to achieve the alterations required to leave.

This view is not without difficulty, however. The most important problem concerns the notion of possibility to which Swinburne's argument appeals. Although there may be some sense of 'impossible' on which persons as described by Swinburne find it impossible to choose the good, the sense in question is not that involved in (H3), the claim that getting out of hell is impossible. We have not to this point addressed the issue of what sense of 'impossible' is involved in (H3), but one clear requirement on a proper understanding of the notion is that it leave no room for God or anyone else to change one's eternal residence. There are two ways to secure this result. The first way construes (H3) in terms of metaphysical impossibility, and the second in terms of accidental impossibility. The first kind of impossibility concerns that which, in the broadest logical sense, cannot occur. For example, a prime number between one and two is metaphysically impossible. The primary examples of accidental impossibility concern the prospects for changing the past. It is impossible in the accidental sense to bring it about that Caesar never crossed the Rubicon or to bring it about that Hitler never invaded Poland. Interpreted in the first way, Swinburne's suggestion does not imply the truth of (H3). A clear indication that the notion of possibility involved in Swinburne's discussion is not metaphysical possibility is that it is subject to becoming: What used to be possible (the choice of the good) is no longer possible. Metaphysical possibility, however, is not subject to becoming; nothing comes to be metaphysically possible that was not possible in the past, and nothing ceases to be metaphysically possible that was possible in the past. So, clearly, Swinburne's remarks about the loss of a soul cannot show that (H3) is true.

This argument leads naturally into the second alternative, for whereas metaphysical impossibility is not subject to becoming, it is of the very nature of accidental impossibility to change over time. Our initial understanding of being accidentally necessary construes it in terms of those claims that are about the past; for example, *Caesar crossed the Rubicon* is accidentally necessary because it is about the past and no one, not even God, can change the past (this last remark is somewhat controversial, but assuming it does not affect further discussion). Using this notion of necessity, we can say that what was only possible and not necessary can become necessary, and what used to be possible is possible no longer. Perhaps by employing this notion of necessity, Swinburne's argument for rejecting (H4) will imply the truth of (H3).

Such is not the case, however. Our understanding of what is accidentally necessary requires that what is accidentally necessary or impossible is expressed by a past-tense sentence. In our example, the claim about the crossing of the Rubicon by Caesar is accidentally necessary because we express that claim by the sentence "Caesar crossed the Rubicon." Yet, Swinburne claims that what is impossible is the *present and future* choosing of the good, and because this impossibility attaches to a claim about the present and future rather than to one about the past, there is no good reason to think that it is accidental impossibility. Swinburne might reply that something in the present or future can be accidentally impossible by virtue of being logically implied by claims about the past that are accidentally impossible, but this attempt cannot rescue the position. The fact that one has lost the power to choose the good does not logically imply that at present one cannot choose the good. All that might follow is that the power to choose the good would require some sort of divine intervention to restore what has been lost.

This last remark suggests a way for Swinburne to defend his view: to maintain that it is not the choosing of the good that is metaphysically impossible, but rather the choosing of the good *without divine intervention*. That is, without some intervention that results in a person's no longer being in the state Swinburne describes, choosing the good is metaphysically impossible. Talbott's earlier argument is to the point regarding this suggestion. His argument claims that a loving God would remove interfering factors that prevent a person from choosing the good. Even if a person is in such a predicament that choosing the good is not possible for that person to choose the good while in that predicament, it does not follow that it is impossible (in a sense required for the truth of (H4)) for that person to get out of hell. All that follows is that, apart from divine intervention, hell is inescapable. In the end, Swinburne must hold that at some point God simply abandons persons to the consequences of their free actions, for nothing in his account explains how, once it becomes impossible for a person to choose the good, the issue of place of residence for eternity is closed. Yet Swinburne never argues for the moral acceptability of this abandonment, and thus his reasoning is incomplete. In any case, if his account is to prove acceptable, more must be said than what he has given us.

The important lesson here is not the weakness of Swinburne's position, but rather the way in which a rejection of (H4) seems to call for further rejections of other elements of the strong view of hell. A natural response to this last objection is simply to point out that Swinburne has no need to defend the No Escape Thesis. He does not suggest this denial, but others are more explicit in tying a rejection of the Retributive Thesis to a denial of the No Escape Thesis. C. S. Lewis, for example, says,

> I willingly believe that the damned are, in one sense, successful, rebels to the end; that the doors of hell are locked on the *inside*. I do not mean that the ghosts may not *wish* to come out of hell, in the vague

fashion wherein an envious man "wishes" to be happy: but they certainly do not will even the first preliminary stages of that self-abandonment through which alone the soul can reach any good. They enjoy forever the horrible freedom they have demanded, and are therefore self-enslaved: just as the blessed, forever submitting to obedience, become through all eternity more and more free.[34]

Lewis's position differs from Swinburne's in that Lewis never suggests that a person's character can become of such a nature that the person is totally intractable. He explicitly rejects the claim of (H3) that one cannot get out of hell once one is there. Instead of maintaining the Retributive Thesis, Lewis substitutes for it, as does Swinburne, a Self-Incarceration Thesis, according to which an eternal stay in hell is the direct result only of the choices one makes, rather than a result imposed by some other power such as God.

Other alternatives to the Retributive Thesis are also possible. For example, one could hold a quarantine model, in which sinners are isolated from the blessed in heaven to avoid infecting the heavenly community with the disease of sin. Eleanore Stump holds, for example, that one reason for the creation of hell is to prevent bad people from harming the innocent.[35] She couples this rejection of (H4) with a rejection of the No Escape Thesis, maintaining instead that it is only a contingent fact that no one ever leaves hell.

Note that the common ways of rejecting (H4) usually are coupled with further rejections of elements of the strong view of hell, which is important for two reasons. First, it shows that the attempt to construct a simple alternative to the strong view by abandoning only (H4) is difficult to sustain, and our discussion has shown that the ways that have been attempted to this point do not succeed. There is a more important lesson, however. I began this chapter by pointing out the way in which the strong view of hell involves features that constitute the "hard core" of a sustained effort to solve the problem of hell, for the typical alternatives to the strong view propose a simple alternative to that view. We have seen, however, that a simple alternative that rejects only (H4) is most difficult to find; in short, the arguments I have put forward have been directed in large part at positions of straw rather than of flesh and blood. The lesson, I suggest, is that the "hard core" of the strong view of hell is precisely (H4). The heart of traditional ways of thinking about hell and attempting to solve the problem of hell builds on the foundation of a retributive model of hell. That is why, when a position denies (H4), the analysis does not stop there but also usually denies other elements of the strong view. Once the hard core of an approach to a problem is denied, other features involved in the traditional approaches to the problem are easily cast aside as well. What I have been arguing for, then, in the last two chapters is this: Not only are the strong view and typical alternatives to it inadequate but also the heart of the approach to the problem of hell that these viewpoints assume is the retributive conception of hell. This hard core needs to be reevaluated, and that effort requires something beyond an approach that attempts to solve the problem of hell by eliminating some supposedly problematic element of the strong view. Such is not the case, and any solution to the problem of hell, I suggest, needs to begin afresh, replacing the hard core of the strong view with a different approach.

Conclusion

The solution to the problem of hell can be found, then, only by finding an acceptable substitute for (H4). The point of the last two chapters is to begin to convince the reader that the usual approaches to the problem of hell founder because they rely on a retributive model of hell. Nothing contained in the last two chapters implies, of course, that a retributive model of hell is mistaken, but the results achieved so far at least serve to bring that model of hell to the forefront in our attempt to grapple with the problem of hell. In the next chapter I begin a more fundamental investigation into the problem of hell than that represented by simple alternatives to the strong view. Should such an approach suggest that the only legitimate core for a doctrine of hell is retributive, the problem of hell would appear insoluble. A more optimistic view is that we might find some other model from which to construct a complete account of the nature of hell. To these issues we now turn.

Notes

1. See "Falsification and the Methodology of Scientific Research Programmes," in *Criticism and the Growth of Knowledge*, edited by Imre Lakatos and Alan Musgrave (Cambridge, 1970).

2. It might as easily be called 'the conditional immortality view', for on this view, immortality is a gift of God to the redeemed. Strictly speaking, the annihilation view differs from the conditional immortality view in that it is compatible with the annihilation view that the soul is intrinsically immortal (though still subject to annihilation by the power of God). For a defense of the conditional immortality view, see Oscar Cullman, *Immortality of the Soul or Resurrection of the Dead?* (New York, 1964). I discuss

the differences between the two views later in this section and argue that they are irrelevant for our purposes.

3. Brian Hebblethwaite, in *The Christian Hope* (Basingstoke, 1984), objects to the strong view of hell by claiming, "Such permanent evil makes no . . . moral sense. . . . It is much more plausible to suppose that the language of damnation and everlasting loss is symbolic language. . . . But if such a terrible possibility is in fact fulfilled, it must mean that the lost one . . . disappears from being" (p. 216). These remarks suggest that Hebblethwaite thinks that the annihilation view is superior on moral grounds to the strong view of hell, for he holds that the annihilation view makes more "moral sense" than does the alternative view maintaining the Eternal Existence Thesis.

Hebblethwaite is not alone in these sentiments. A multitude of examples of the same can be found in D. P. Walker, *The Decline of Hell* (Chicago, 1964).

4. See D. P. Walker, *The Decline of Hell*, especially the Introduction, for an extensive historical discussion of this view.

5. Ibid., p. 4.

6. That exaggerations of the strong view are lies is defended by Walker in *The Decline of Hell*. The accusation of prevarication is not too strong. There is convincing evidence that those who propounded in public the most disturbing views on hell also distinguished (in private) between an *esoteric* and an *exoteric* doctrine: The real truth was only for the enlightened and would be socially disastrous if presented for public consumption. The misrepresentation was not for personal gain, the usual motivation in cases of lying, but the appellation is no less appropriate.

7. Here, as elsewhere in this work, I ignore the difficult problems surrounding an explication of the notion of justice required by the strong view of hell. It is a retributive theory that determines the appropriateness of punishment on the basis of a "fit" between punishment and crime. The difficult problems arise in attempting to explicate this notion of fitness. For purposes of argument, I here grant that an appropriate explication can be found. For even granting this point, the views that rest on such a theory of justice fail.

8. For a historical account of the beginnings of the popularity of universalism, see Walker, *The Decline of Hell*.

9. An exception may be taken here concerning the controversy in England in the eighteenth century surrounding the "Damnatory Clause," Article 43 of the Athanasian Creed, which reads, "And they that have done good shall go into life everlasting; and they that have done evil into everlasting fire." Article 44 reads, "This is the Catholic Faith, which except a man believe faithfully, he cannot be saved." The controversy continued sporadically, and when the Episcopal church in the United States separated from that in England, it deliberately omitted the Athanasian Creed as a standard of faith in ratifying the Prayer Book in 1789. This concern over the Damna-

tory Clause, however, was not so much an affirmation of universalism as a rebellion against the traditional doctrine of hell.

10. Walker, *The Decline of Hell*, especially Part Two, treats the historical figures mentioned.

11. See, for example, Emil Brunner, *Eternal Hope*, trans. by Harold Knight (Philadelphia, 1954); and Karl Barth, *Church Dogmatics* (Edinburgh, 1936–1969) vol. IV, each of whom apparently affirm universalism, but where the stress on 'apparently' must be strong. Others recent theologians given to such tendencies include Karl Rahner, Paul Althaus, and Hans Urs von Balthasar. A notable exception here is John A. T. Robinson's *In the End, God* (New York, 1968), which shows obvious signs of the influence of existential thought and yet clearly embraces a version of universalism.

12. I use Macquarrie as an example, although he disagrees with the afterlife dimension central to my examination of the problem of hell.

13. John Macquarrie, *Principles of Christian Theology* (New York, 1966), p. 327.

14. Ibid., p. 322.

15. Ibid., p. 327.

16. Hans Küng, *Eternal Life?* trans. Edward Quinn (Garden City, N.Y., 1984), pp. 141–142.

17. Clark Pinnock, "Fire, Then Nothing," *Christianity Today*, March 20, 1987, pp. 40–41.

18. Such a position is committed to the possibility of some counterfactuals with necessarily false antecedents failing to be only trivially true, in contrast to what the standard semantics for such counterfactuals implies. The standard semantics for counterfactuals proceeds in terms of finding a "close" world in which the antecedent of a counterfactual is true, where the notion of closeness is a technical notion, the explication of which is deeply problematic. For our purposes, the rough idea is that one world is closer to the actual world than another just in case the first is more like the actual world than the second, in terms of which causal laws are true and which events occur and in what order. Now, if there are no worlds in which the antecedent is true, there will be no close worlds in which the antecedent is true; and, on the semantics in question, a counterfactual is true just in case there is a closer world in which both antecedent and consequent are true to any world where the antecedent is true and the consequent false. Thus, when there are no worlds in which the antecedent is true, the counterfactual is trivially true. For more on the semantics for counterfactuals, see Robert Stalnaker, "A Theory of Conditionals," pp. 165–179, in Ernest Sosa, ed., *Causation and Conditionals* (Oxford, 1975); and David Lewis, *Counterfactuals* (Oxford, 1973).

This commitment of necessary universalism should not be thought damaging to the position, however, for this implication of the standard semantics for counterfactuals is one of the least attractive features of that semantics. Thus, it is appropriate to treat necessary universalism as unscathed in its conflict with the semantics for counterfactuals.

19. Thomas P. Talbott, "The Doctrine of Everlasting Punishment," *Faith and Philosophy* 7.1 (January 1990): 19–43.

20. Ibid., p. 37.

21. Ibid., p. 38.

22. For an account of the relevant notion of subjective rationality, see Richard Foley, *The Theory of Epistemic Rationality* (Cambridge, 1986).

23. If the suffering of the blessed in heaven at the thought of the suffering in hell is to count as a reason in favor of any version of universalism, the present difficulty for universalism presents an equally foreboding problem. If I would suffer by knowing that others are suffering in hell, I would also suffer at knowing either that certain persons were suffering in heaven by being forced to reside there against their will or that their wills were kept placated only by means of some radical reduction of their capacities. Better to solve the problem of how the blessed can be truly blessed while others are in hell than to accept a forced universalism, for suffering in heaven is not in principle different than suffering in hell (although the degree, or quantity, of suffering may differ).

24. Alvin Plantinga, *The Nature of Necessity* (Oxford, 1974), pp. 169–184.

25. Ibid., pp. 180–181.

26. See David Lewis, *Counterfactuals* (Oxford, 1973) for arguments against LCEM.

27. Plantinga, *The Nature of Necessity*, p. 182.

28. See Lewis, *Counterfactuals*, on this point.

29. In Plantinga's terminology, God cannot strongly actualize my freely working on this book, for that would amount to his deterministically causing it to be the case that I do something that is not determined. Plantinga does not explicitly say that the causing must be deterministic, but from his discussion he obviously intends the notion of causing to be such. See *The Nature of Necessity*, pp. 170–174.

30. Ibid., p. 181.

31. Brian Hebblethwaite, *The Christian Hope*, pp. 213–214.

32. In fairness to Hebblethwaite, I should point out that his account is not a simple alternative to the strong view. He seems to deny that the justification for hell is retributive at all, he believes that the wicked will be annihilated, and he hopes that annihilation is only a mere possibility and that all in the end will be saved. Furthermore, he thinks this hope is reasonable. See *The Christian Hope*, chapter 11, for an exposition of these views.

33. Richard Swinburne, "A Theodicy of Heaven and Hell," in *The Existence and Nature of God*, ed. Alfred J. Freddoso (Notre Dame, 1983), pp. 48–49.

34. C. S. Lewis, *The Problem of Pain* (London, 1973), pp. 115–116.

35. Eleonore Stump, "Dante's Hell, Aquinas's Moral Theory, and the Love of God," *Canadian Journal of Philosophy* 16 (1986): 181–196.

3

The Issuant Conception of Hell

In a recent philosophy of religion class, a student queried why, on usual theistic conceptions, God's desire that we share eternity with him does not violate the Kantian moral requirement not to treat persons as a mere means to one's own ends. I responded by outlining the usual theistic reply to this question, that sharing eternity with God is the best thing that could happen to anyone, and one does not treat a person as a mere means to one's own ends when one is pursuing what is best for that person. This reply left another student troubled. His immediate response was, "But why does he get so angry, then, when we just want to be left alone?" This question succinctly summarizes a host of problems that arise on the standard conception of hell, problems ranging from some apparent vindictiveness on the part of God when sending someone to hell, to an inadequate account of why there is no third alternative, perhaps less blessed than heaven but more convenient than hell. What is most important about the question, however, is not the range of problems it raises, but something deeper. The heart of the question centers on the picture of God's motivations as presented by Christians who hold a traditional conception of hell in explaining presence in heaven versus presence in hell. The question is rooted in perplexity as to why there is such a dramatic shift from the motivation of love in the one case to the motivation of retribution or vindictiveness in the other.

Not just bright undergraduates find such a shift troubling. The discussion of universalism in the last chapter cited several theologians who have thought that the fact that God is a loving God calls for a rejection of traditional views of hell. More recently, Marilyn Adams has complained that most Christians have assumed incorrectly that justice is God's fundamental moral characteristic in describing hell.[1] Thomas Talbott has given, moreover, a rigorous defense of the claim that one cannot maintain traditional views of hell if one has a deep appreciation for God's love for all humanity.[2] Furthermore, traditional Christianity has done little to quell the concern. Beginning with the condemnation of universalism at the Fifth General Council at Constantinople in 553 A.D., through the vivid imagery contained in Jonathan Edwards's "Sinners in the Hands of an Angry God," to contemporary discussion, something other than God's love and grace has been the focus when the doctrine of hell is addressed. Augustine's discussion of the matter is a classic example of this tendency:.

> Now, who but a fool would think God unfair either when he imposes penal judgment on the deserving or when he shows mercy to the undeserving? . . . [T]he whole human race was condemned in its apostate head by a divine judgment so just that even if not a single member of the race were ever saved from it, no one could rail against God's justice.[3]

Here the student's question is probing. Traditional Christian theology describes God's purposes for humanity initially in terms of his love for us. Yet when humanity is uncooperative, Christians appeal to God's justice to account for the condemnation that results. But why the shift from love to justice? Christians often respond to questions about hell by claiming that God is not only a loving God but also perfectly just and holy. That response, however, is not an answer to the problem underlying the student's question. It only illustrates it.

Christian discussions often cause even more consternation, for they not only appeal inexplicably to a different motivational structure in explaining hell than the account that makes love God's dominant motive when accounting for heaven, but also seem positively at odds with God's continuing to love certain persons when acting out of justice toward them. Aquinas says, "God loves every man, and every creature also, in that he wills some good for every one of them. But he does not will every good for every one, and is said to hate some in so far as he does not will for them the good of eternal life."[4] Note that willing some good for a person is not sufficient for loving that person; at bottom, Aquinas seems to hold that God does not love those to whom he does not grant eternal life.

Or consider what can appear to be an ascription of callousness by God toward his creation: "For God a billion rational creatures are as dust in the balance; if a billion perish, God suffers no loss, who can create what he wills with no effort or cost by merely thinking of it."[5] Even worse is the position taken by the nineteenth century Reformed theologian Herman Hoeksema, who, according to Talbott, held that God truly loves only a limited elect, whereas the nonelect are subject to the "sovereign hatred of God."[6]

Talbott calls the position that denies that God loves all created persons the position of *hard-hearted theism*. He argues that this position is false, for God cannot really love some persons without loving them all.[7] My intent here is not to address the philosophical or theological merits of hard-hearted theism, but let me at least register my view that Talbott's argument is successful against the view. My point here is rather *procedural*; my aim is to draw attention to a perplexing feature common to traditional Christian discussions of hell: Whereas God's love and grace predominate in a discussion of heaven, the focus shifts completely when turning to the topic of hell.

Given the background context these discussions of hell present, this student's question is rhetorically powerful. More important for the present chapter, however, is that the question provides for us a powerful diagnostic tool. A great divide lies between the type of presentation one finds of the strong view of hell and many of the simple alternatives to it. The standard heresies concerning hell usually focus on God's loving nature and claim that, when describing the ultimate character of hell, more attention must be paid to the loving character of God. More traditional conceptions of hell standardly appeal to divergent aspects of God's character in explaining heaven and hell. Heaven is usually explained by God's love, but hell is explained by God's justice. Where the heresies find unity and stability in God's motivational structure, orthodoxy has often given accounts that offer a picture of variability and inconstancy.

I want to draw a moral from the distinction between these two approaches, but first we need to understand clearly what is at stake between them. Explaining some of God's actions by appealing to one of his characteristics and different divine actions by appealing to other characteristics is not in itself a mistake. Of course, the present case is not simply an example of two different actions by God. Instead, in the present case, we have two different actions that are mutually exclusive and jointly exhaustive of the logically possible actions that might be performed. That is, the disposition of our case by God must be, according to Christianity, either to consign one to hell or welcome one into heaven. Not even in this case would it be untoward to cite different motives for one action than for another. Instead, my complaint is that it is not enough *merely* to cite different motives. We must also have some account of how the different motives are related to each other.

This last point can be illustrated by a case of fully deliberate and reflective human action. Suppose Sam both wants to eat ice cream and wants to avoid gaining weight, and is considering whether to eat some ice cream. After deliberating, he chooses. In such a case, we cannot have explanations of the competing actions that appeal only to the related desire. That is, supposing he chooses ice cream, an adequate explanation of this choice is not to point out that he has a strong desire to eat ice cream. After all, such an explanation ignores the deliberative character of his action. Instead, the explanation would have to cite, in addition to the strength of desire, the views Sam achieves by deliberating about what course of action would be best. That is, his deliberation results in some order of priority for his desires, and this ordering is also part of the explanation of his action.

So there are two ways to try to explain Sam's possible actions: one that combines or synthesizes the desires that pull Sam in different directions and another that focuses myopically on only the desire that is satisfied by Sam's action. The lesson to be learned is that adequate explanations in certain contexts need to cite the way in which the competing forces contribute to the final vector of action. We might call this kind of explanation an *integrated* explanation of action, and the alternative a *segregated* explanation. Sam's behavior arises in a context that calls for an integrated explanation of his action.

We are now in a position to see why the student's question is a useful diagnostic tool. It shows that the depictions of hell with which he is familiar diverge in their explanations of heaven and hell in such a way that they constitute segregated explanations of heaven and hell. The heart of his concern is an unexplained shift from one account of the divine motivation to another in the discussion of the two ultimate options in the afterlife. Traditional Christian accounts of hell begin by characterizing God's fundamental desire in relation to humanity as a desire for union with human beings, but in the discussion of hell, this portrayal is abandoned. No longer does love seem to be part of the picture at all; instead, God's dominant motive is portrayed in terms of justice (at best) or vindictiveness (at worst). Moreover, usually nothing is added to assuage the concern that this shifting of motivational bases for action is more befitting the mentally incompetent than the fully rational.

Of course, I am not claiming that this lack in traditional presentations of hell cannot be remedied. I am claiming, however, that any account of hell that involves such a shift and does not explain it is theoretically inadequate. Furthermore, the needed explanation cannot posit a change in the character of God, for example, from being an individual whose primary motive is love to one whose primary motive is justice. Such changes of character are possible for imperfect beings, but God's character is not alterable in this way, according to traditional theism. The difficulty I am pointing out may be only pedagogical in that there may be an explanation for the shift that traditional Christianity has failed regularly to present. Without a satisfactory explanation, however, a theoretical thorn is in the flesh of traditional Christianity.

One way to hide the need for a combined account of heaven and hell involves a shift in perspective, but note that this shift in no way solves the problem I am raising. If we pursue a parent-child analogy, there are two perspectives to take on any situation in which a parent makes a request or command. From the parent's perspective, satisfying the request or following the command is important for the good of the child. Thus, we might say, the request or command arises from the love the parent has for the child. Suppose, however, that the child refuses to satisfy the request or obey the command; how should we explain the resulting behavior of the parent? One way is to shift to the child's perspective and note that, because the child fully understood the request or command and knew of the obligation created by it, it is fully just and wholly proper for the parents to discipline the child for violating the obligation.

This very shift in perspective may lead to the perplexity caused by the student's query; that is, in describing heaven, the divine perspective may be assumed, whereas in describing hell the human perspective is taken up. When this shift in perspective goes unnoticed, it begins to appear that heaven arises out of God's graciousness and hell out of his severity.

If this shift is the underlying cause of the appearance that traditional accounts of heaven and hell are segregated accounts, the remedy is not found in pointing out the cause. The remedy is found instead in presenting an account that resists the temptation to shift perspectives.

Of course, remedying this defect of traditional accounts of hell will not rescue anything like the strong view of hell, for, as we have seen, there is much more wrong with the strong view of hell than that it is normally part of a segregated account of heaven and hell. I suggest that a lesson we can learn from the student's question is that any adequate account of hell must begin with an understanding of the nature of God and present the possibilities of heaven and hell as flowing from this one nature; that is, a solution to the problem of hell can be obtained only by an integrated account of heaven and hell. One way to satisfy this condition of adequacy is to offer an account of heaven and hell in which the very same characteristics of God generate both alternatives. Another way is to locate the existence of each in separate divine attributes and give some explanation as to why the attribute generating hell must predominate when the attribute generating heaven cannot.[8]

I shall call a conception of hell that is part of an account of heaven and hell that satisfies this condition of adequacy an "issuant conception of hell." We can begin the task of developing an issuant conception of hell by investigating those parts of God's nature relevant to the doctrine of hell.

The Nature of God

It might appear a truism that, according to Christianity, the doctrines of heaven and hell are rooted most deeply in God's goodness; that is, it might appear completely obvious that, in the Christian view, God's love and beneficence are his fundamental character traits, for Christians cite these traits when describing why God created anything at all and, most important, why God sent Jesus on his redemptive mission. Taking God's goodness to be fundamental might then seem unassailable, but we cannot begin our discussion here, for there is a strong tradition in Christian theology that explains things otherwise. According to many Christian theologians, what is fundamental is that God is completely and absolutely sovereign, not subject to anything outside himself. A natural accompaniment to this view is that God's only duty, if it can be called such, is to bring glory to himself. In the words of Théodore de Bèze,

> God has created the world for His glory; His glory is not known, unless His mercy and His justice are declared: to this end He has, as an act of sheer grace, destined some men to eternal life, and some, by just judgment, to eternal damnation. Mercy presupposes misery, justice presupposes guilt.[9]

The view expressed here is that God's ultimate goal of glorifying himself is served best by saving some and damning others, for only by saving some and damning others can his mercy and justice "be declared." As an argument, these remarks are especially weak. God could have made his justice known in a multitude of ways without damning anyone to hell. Perhaps, even, his justice could have been inferred a priori from the nature of the divine character without any experiential "declaration" at all.

Nonetheless, the position expressed in this quote represents a strong tradition in theology, one in which these remarks are quite benign. More malignant are remarks such as those of Pierre Jurieu, who claims that even if the theological tradition that emphasizes God's glory above all else "shows us a cruel, unjust God punishing and chastising innocent creatures with eternal torments," this position is not objectionable because

> it raises the Divine to the highest degree of greatness and superiority that can be conceived. For it abases the creature before the Creator to such a point, that in this system the Creator is bound by no sort of law with regard to the creature, but can do with it as seems good to Him, and make it serve His glory in any way He pleases, without its having the right to gainsay Him.[10]

As I implied, this account of God's sovereignty is especially unsettling. Nevertheless, it arises quite easily from thoroughly unimpeachable theological motives. Such accounts arise from a desire to maintain the absolute supremacy of God over all there is or could be. God himself is ultimately responsible for anything that exists, and there is nothing to which God is responsible or upon which God depends. The desire to maintain these central aspects of monotheism, however, must be combined with a philosophical account of the relationship between God and whatever (other) necessary existents there are, such as (perhaps) propositions, properties, relations, and mathematical and logical truths. Most important, an account is needed of the relationship between God and morality. Here things take a turn for the worse, for some find themselves in the position of thinking that in order for God to be above all else and subject to nothing else, he must be above morality itself, perhaps above it in such a way that he does things that anyone subject to the demands of morality would not be allowed to do. A position such as that of Jurieu highlights in the greatest possible way the superiority of God above his creation and the conceptual distance between creator and creature.

The most obvious and crippling defect of this position is that it eliminates the possibility of allowing the judgment that God is perfectly good to have any content to it. If God is beyond morality, then nothing God does can be truly said to be evil, or bad, or unjust. The price of this conclusion is inordinately high, however, for it can equally be pointed out that, if God is above morality, then nothing God does can be correctly said to be good, or right, or just; that is, these things cannot be said unless one stipulates that goodness is to be understood in terms of whatever God does. If one takes this route, it is true that God is good and perfectly so; the problem is that it is a trivial truth, no more informative about God's character and behavior than is the statement that God is God.

The mistake that leads to these problems arises not in the desire to preserve the sovereignty of God, which has a long and impressive tradition in monotheistic thought, but in the philosophical understanding of the relationship between God and necessary existents. The inference that the views shown here presuppose is that necessary existents are somehow a threat to the sovereignty of God. However, this position is far from indisputable, and the reprehensible repercussions of it argue strongly in favor of pursuing conceptions of the relationship between God and necessity that do not threaten sovereignty. Recent discussion has argued that even if there are objects that cannot fail to exist, it does not follow that they do not depend on God for their existence.[11] Equally important to note is that God's goodness does not depend on his following moral rules that bind him in the way in which moral rules bind human beings. Although exploring the view in depth would take us too far afield, a few clarifying remarks might prove useful. According to traditional theism, God is perfectly and essentially good, and part of being perfectly good is failing to violate the requirements of morality. However, that God is bound by the principles of morality in the way we are, or subject to them, does not follow from this fact. Central to the relationship we have to morality is the capacity both to do what is right and to do what is wrong. In this way, morality stands above us and over us, and imposes judgments on us when we fail to do what is right. Yet, because God is necessarily good, he is not subject to morality in this way. He fulfills the demands of morality perfectly and necessarily; in fact, his goodness is so exemplary that doing anything wrong is impossible for God. Hence, morality does not bind him in the way it binds us.[12]

In this account of God's goodness, the uprightness of his moral character is preserved without sacrificing any of the content of such a judgment: God does what would be required of any individual subject to the demands of morality in his situation. This account may appear to have too high a price, however, for it appears to imply that God is not praiseworthy for doing right. If God does not choose to do what is right but does it of necessity, praising him for doing what is right would seem to be no longer appropriate. Even if persons who do their duty can be properly praised for doing right, praise would seem to be inappropriate unless they had other options. This worry can be allayed, however, for even if this conception of God sacrifices his praiseworthiness for doing right, a multitude of avenues are still open to one who wishes to preserve the praiseworthiness of God. God's goodness, according to Christianity, is not exhausted by his satisfying whatever obligations a person bound by morality would have in his situation; his goodness is superabundant in terms of the unmerited and unrequired blessings that he bestows. According to Christianity, creation itself is a mark of God's goodness, not an action he is required to perform. Furthermore, the blessings both temporal and eternal that God gives to his creatures out of love for them also display his goodness. His praiseworthiness can still be defended by rooting it in the way his goodness overflows the bounds of even the most stringent of the plausible moral systems. He is praiseworthy for his love, his grace, and his unmerited favor, even if he is not, strictly speaking, praiseworthy for not violating the demands of morality.[13]

The upshot of this discussion is that the theological tradition that seeks to emphasize God's sovereignty at the expense of morality, as the remarks of Jurieu do, must be abandoned. Its motivations are not suspect, for it seeks to retain the traditional theistic claim that God is the hub on which the wheel of all else turns and that there is nothing on which God depends. The mistake is philosophical rather than motivational. It is in thinking that, if God depends on nothing other than himself, then the demands of morality need not accurately describe his behavior. If they did, so the thinking goes, God would be answerable to moral principles and so would be subject to and dependent on them. We have no reason to accept this line of thinking, and the price for accepting it is the doctrine of the goodness of God. The proper conclusion to draw is that this form of the tradition that emphasizes the sovereignty of God is truly malignant.

There is still the benign form, however, according to which God's purposes in creation—and the only requirement to which he might be held accountable—is to glorify himself. He does not do this by violating any moral principles, but (according to this tradition) he is not to be judged by human standards concerning kindness, compassion, concern for others, or the like. He is simply not answerable to us in this way; he is answerable only to himself and to his purpose of bringing glory to himself.

It must be admitted at the outset that something is strikingly perverse about this conception of God's motivational structure. In it, God seems inordinately self-interested and self-centered, even egocentric. One way out of this charge is to claim that God is interested in displaying his glory *for our benefit;* that is, he desires to manifest his glory because he is the most excellent thing there is or could be and his desire for us is that we have and appreciate the best. This answer grounds God's display of his glory in his love, but this response is not available to the position under discussion, which insists that God's purposes are to be clarified solely in terms of his goal of glorifying himself. This purpose is not ancillary to others, but primary, for it is the sole purpose to which his actions are answerable. Because of this emphasis, the theological tradition in question, even in its benign form, cannot avoid at least the appearance that this theology is of an egocentric being.

It might be thought that this charge can be answered by pointing out that, because God is the highest good, his love of himself and desire to glorify himself cannot be inordinate. Such is not the case, however. It is true that God cannot have an inordinate love of himself, but even if he is the highest good, it does not follow that a desire to glorify himself cannot be inordinate. Part of being the highest good involves the self-giving nature of God to love that which he has created. Yet, to bestow benefits on an individual for the sake of one's own glorification surely does not count as love. To truly love someone requires being motivated fundamentally by the welfare of the one loved. Hence, even though God's love of himself cannot be inordinate, the theological tradition in question is still plagued with the problem of making God out to be unduly egocentric.

To appreciate how this tradition lands itself in this predicament is not difficult. The motivation is, once again, to preserve the majesty, greatness, and sovereignty of God against all else. To do so, this tradition feels that God must be answerable to no one but himself (which may be granted) and that if God's purposes are other than his own self-glorification he is answerable in a problematic way to someone other than himself (which should not be granted). Once again, we find admirable motives combined with inadequate reasoning underlying this tradition.

The fundamental weakness of this system is that it is so interested in preserving the sovereignty of God that it seeks to construe God's sovereignty by developing a theological system in which God is immune from criticism. The best way for Christians to achieve that goal, however, is to defend the perfect goodness of God. A Christian view of God's goodness implies not only that God satisfies perfectly the demands of morality (and so makes God immune from criticism) but also that God is gracious, bestowing blessings beyond the bound of any legitimate moral demands.

The conclusion to be drawn, then, is that when discussing the Christian view of the relationship between God and his creation the most important divine characteristic to consider is his goodness. In this view, God's behavior in creating and his behavior toward his creation are rooted in his goodness. His goodness, however, is not a simple characteristic. As we have seen, part of God's goodness involves his perfectly satisfying the requirements of morality, and another part, his loving beneficence, is involved in the story of creation. In addition, his love is an aspect of his goodness that is displayed toward his creation primarily, according to Christianity, in the incarnation itself and its eternal effects. In the context of a discussion of the problem of hell, however, we would be remiss to fail to mention that justice is a necessary feature of God's goodness as well. As already noted, God violates none of the demands of morality, and some of these demands are demands for justice.

Once we get both love and justice into the picture, however, we cannot avoid a segregated account of heaven and hell unless we explain how the two are related to each other in accounting both for presence in heaven and for presence in hell. The important question we must face here is which of the two is dominant. Is God primarily motivated in terms of love, where this love is constrained in some way by justice, or is God primarily motivated by justice?

Nicolas Malebranche held the latter view. According to him, justice is God's supreme moral attribute, with all others being wholly subordinate to it and derived from it. He claims that God "is neither clement, nor merciful, nor good, according to vulgar notions, since He is just both essentially, and by the natural and necessary love He bears to His divine perfections."[14] For Malebranche, every aspect of the relationship between God and his creation is based on considerations of justice.

This view has important weaknesses. Most important, accounting for creation itself is difficult if justice is God's primary motivational characteristic. The type of justice in question—retributive justice—is reactive rather than active or creative. Justice leads us to respond to situations that already have occurred and to individuals who already exist. To creatively bring into being is more naturally accounted for in terms of love or self-giving. One does not, for example, intentionally procreate out of a sense of justice; procreation is morally exemplary instead when it arises out of a desire to give of oneself to another.

At this point Malebranche fudges the issue a bit in order to be able to account for creation. He maintains that God loves himself and thereby can only act with the ultimate purpose of glorifying himself. This position may help account for why God created anything at all, but it is hard to reconcile with the viewpoint that justice is God's primary characteristic. My purpose, however, is not to become embroiled in details of Malebranche's thought, but to point out that some explanation must be given for creation itself other than one founded in justice. Malebranche's explanation harks to a tradition I rejected previously, one that cites God's desire to glorify himself as his primary motivational characteristic. More important, however, any new ground posited to explain creation will be inconsistent with the viewpoint that God's fundamental motivational characteristic is justice. Given the dialectical position we have achieved, we cannot accept Malebranche's alternative account and thus are left only with the view that God's love and desire to give of self underlie creation. We are left, that is, with the view that God's fundamental motivational characteristic is love.

This conclusion fits well the claims of Christianity. The position that God's justice is more fundamental than his love seems in direct opposition to the heart of Christianity, because the biblical picture of God is that of one who continually postpones the visitation of justice in favor of demonstrations of love. If his justice were dominant, God could have no reason to postpone immediate recompense for wrongdoing, although he might in his love and mercy have some reason to apply the least severe punishment compatible with his just and holy nature. He also could have no reason, in the words of St. Paul (via the King James translators), to send his Son in the likeness of human flesh to reconcile the world unto himself. Having a reason for such an action requires that his love be the dominant motivational force in his interaction with human beings and that satisfying the demands of his just and holy nature be conformed to this dominant, fundamental characteristic.

These remarks are not limited to the Christian tradition within theism. Any religion has difficulty maintaining that God is dominated by a concern for justice if that religion claims there is a human predicament for which humans are responsible rather than God and that God has undertaken to resolve. Undertaking the resolution of the predicament cannot be explained in terms of the demands of justice. Thus, it would seem that in any reasonable theistic picture of which Christianity is a type, love as opposed to justice must be the fundamental motivation of God in dealing with humanity.

I am not suggesting for a moment that an adequate Christian account implies that God *violates* his just and holy nature in order to lavish his grace, love, and mercy on us. Instead, I am claiming that God's fundamental attitude toward human beings is one of love and that this conclusion is especially fitting in that the redemption story at the heart of Christianity is a story of God's conforming the demands of justice and holiness to his love. I am arguing for a hierarchical conception of the divine motivations, where God's love is his fundamental motivation regarding human beings and according to which God expends great effort to satisfy the demands of justice and holiness without abandoning that love for us.

It will not do, then, in describing hell, to turn this order on its head and argue in a way that suggests that God's just and holy nature is what is fixed and that he tries to find a way to fit a little love into the picture at the same time. Instead, we need an account of hell in conformity with the claim that it issues out of the same picture of the divine nature that holds forth the blessings of heaven as the highest and perfect gift for human beings.

The God of Love and the Nature of Hell

In the next chapter, I shall present what I consider to be the best issuant conception of hell available. In preparation for that chapter, let us consider some accounts of the nature of hell that are issuant conceptions, for these accounts present in a useful way the difficulties that must be addressed by an adequate issuant conception of hell. Two such accounts were first encountered in the last chapter. In discussing the simple alternative that gives up the Retribution Thesis of the strong view, we discussed briefly Stump's quarantine model of hell, the reformatory model of Swinburne, and the view of C. S. Lewis. I shall not devote any extended discussion to the reformatory model of Swinburne for several reasons. First, we discussed his position at considerable length in the last chapter. Second, we saw there that his position suffered from defects concerning the connection between the reformatory model and the No Escape Thesis. In particular, his viewpoint has difficulty explaining how God still loves those in hell, given that he has apparently irrevocably rejected them. It is open to Swinburne to supplement his account by rejecting the No Escape Thesis in addition to the Retribution Thesis. As things stand, however, he does not do so, which makes it most appropriate to treat his view as a simple alternative to the strong view of hell. Having moved beyond such proposals, I shall here focus discussion on the views of Lewis and Stump, which we mentioned only in passing in the last chapter.

Lewis's Conception of Hell

As we saw in the last chapter, Lewis believes that the doors of hell are locked from the inside rather than from the outside. Thus, according to Lewis, if escape from hell never happens, it is not because God is not willing that it should happen. Instead, residence in hell is eternal because that is just what persons in hell have chosen for themselves. They may "wish" to get out of hell in much the same way as a hardened criminal wishes to avoid prison, but they will not—they choose not—to take the first steps toward self-abandonment required in order to leave their prison.

In the present context, the most important aspect of Lewis's view is his understanding of how the reality of hell flows from the divine nature.

> Supposing he *will* not be converted, what destiny in the eternal world can you regard as proper for him? Can you really desire that such a man, *remaining what he is* . . . should be confirmed forever in his present happiness . . . ? And if you cannot regard this as tolerable, is it only your wickedness—only spite—that prevents you from doing so? Or do you find that conflict between Justice and Mercy, which has sometimes seemed to you such an outmoded piece of theology, now actually at work in your own mind, and feeling very much as if it came to you from above, not from below? You are moved not by a desire for the wretched creature's pain as such, but by a truly ethical demand that, soon or late, the right should be asserted, the flag planted in this horribly rebellious soul, even if no fuller and better conquest is to follow.[15]

According to Lewis, God's love extends as far as it possibly can, until any further extension of it would violate his justice. Hell, then, is what results when love can extend no further without being accompanied by injustice.

Lewis's view, however, is not simply that a person in hell has an inordinately settled will opposed to God. Instead, according to Lewis, the person becomes something quite beyond hope. In discussing the relationship between a retributive conception of hell and a conception according to which the judgment of hell consists in the fact that people prefer darkness to light, Lewis says,

> We are therefore at liberty . . . to think of this bad man's perdition not as a sentence imposed on him but as the mere fact of being what he is. . . . Our imaginary egoist has tried to turn everything he meets into a province or appendage of the self. The taste for the *other*, that is, the very capacity for enjoying good, is quenched in him except in so far as his body still draws him into some rudimentary contact with an outer world. Death removes this last contact. He has his wish—to live wholly in the self and to make the best of what he finds there.[16]

Or again,

> To enter heaven is to become more human than you ever succeeded in being in earth; to enter hell, is to be banished from humanity. What is cast (or casts itself) into hell is not a man: it is "remains." To be a complete man means to have the passions obedient to the will and the will offered to God: to *have been* a man—to be an ex-man or "damned ghost"—would presumably mean to consist of a will utterly centred in its self and passions utterly uncontrolled by the will.[17]

These remarks are echoed by Swinburne in his discussion of the prospect of "losing one's soul." In the process of being given that at which the sinner's life has aimed, the humanity of the sinner is destroyed; what is left are the "remains" of a person. According to both Swinburne and Lewis, this state involves the complete surrendering of the will to the passions, so that, as Swinburne puts it, there is no "he" left to choose the good over what is most strongly desired.

These last remarks complicate the picture that can be painted of Lewis's view, but they also have another effect. They raise an insoluble difficulty for Lewis. This problem concerns Lewis's reasons for rejecting the annihilation conception of hell. Much of what he says suggests the annihilation view, for he holds that what is in hell are the "remains" of a person. Yet, he believes that annihilation is not possible, for he says,

> Destruction, we should naturally assume, means the unmaking, or cessation, of the destroyed. And people often talk as if the "annihilation" of a soul were intrinsically possible. In all our experience, however, the destruction of one thing means the emergence of something else. Burn a log, and you have gases, heat and ash. To *have been* a log means now being those three things. If a soul can be destroyed, must there not be a state of *having been* a human soul? And is not that, perhaps, the state which is equally well described as torment, destruction, and privation?[18]

Lewis's argument here is that true annihilation of anything cannot really occur. There is always something that has the property of having been what it formerly was, and hence the destruction of the soul cannot amount to literal annihilation. If the soul were literally annihilated, there would be nothing that has the property of having been a soul. Hence hell must be a domain of "remains" of persons, rather than a description of the nonexistence of the damned.

This argument, however, is deeply flawed. For one thing, it is incompatible with one version of the Christian doctrine of *creatio ex nihilo*, the doctrine according to which God created the universe literally out of nothing. Lewis claims that every change is the change of something into something else, for he claims that there is always the property of having been what it formerly was. Yet, if we suppose a first moment of time at which God created all that existed at that time out of nothing, there is no such property. The initial state of the universe could not have been, consistent with the doctrine of *creatio ex nihilo*, the creation of something that has the property of having been something else at a previous time.

The mistake Lewis makes is that of confusing what can occur according to scientific law (in particular, the law of conservation according to which mass/energy is conserved in closed systems in every physical interaction) with what can occur in the broader sense of logical or metaphysical possibility. According to traditional theism, God is omnipotent, and one of the implications of this doctrine is that God has the power to destroy the entire created order, leaving absolutely nothing in its place, just as he had the power to call what there is into existence out of nothing.

Not only is Lewis's argument against the annihilation view inadequate but also his response to one objection comes exceedingly close to implying the annihilation view. The objection concerns how the blessed in heaven can be truly blessed while some are suffering in hell, and in response Lewis says,

> But I notice that Our Lord, while stressing the terror of hell with unsparing severity usually emphasises the idea not of duration but of *finality*. Consignment to the destroying fire is usually treated as the end of the story—not as the beginning of a new story. . . . We know much more about heaven than hell, for heaven is the home of humanity and therefore contains all that is implied in a glorified human life: but hell was not made for men. It is in no sense *parallel* to heaven: it is "the darkness outside," the outer rim where being fades away into nonentity.[19]

Yet, if hell does not involve "duration," if it is "in no sense *parallel to heaven*," but instead is "the outer rim where being fades away into nonentity," the most natural view of hell to hold is that it is a metaphorical description of what becomes of a person whom God annihilates. Lewis, however, balks at this conclusion, as we have seen before. Nonetheless, his language is strongly suggestive of that view, and it is not clear how to reinterpret his language so that the annihilation view can be avoided and yet his claims constitute a response to the objection he is considering.

None of this is intended to affirm that the annihilation view is correct. Instead, I am only attempting to determine whether Lewis's account of hell can be maintained. In spite of its many virtues, not the least of which is that it counts as an issuant conception of hell, it cannot be sustained as it stands because it is internally incoherent. Lewis gives a flawed argument against the annihilation position while also relying on something very close to the annihilation position in responding to an objection to hell. Because of this fault, Lewis's position must be rejected. We turn now to consider a different account offered by Stump.

Stump's Quarantine Conception of Hell

Stump offers an account of hell relying on Aquinas's conception of love.[20] She summarizes this view of love as follows: "put roughly, according to Aquinas, love is a passion that stimulates the lover to desire the good of what he loves and recognizes as good and that results in some sort of oneness between the lover and the object of his love."[21] As Aquinas puts it in abbreviated form, to love a person is to will that person good.[22] Thus, in loving us, God does what is open to him to ensure the most good for us.

What is the good in question? Aquinas's answer is the promotion of our rationality, which may seem like an overly cognitive approach to how to love others, but, given some other views of Aquinas, it may not be. Aquinas identifies rational action with moral action, so to aim at the actualization of the capacity to reason is to aim at promoting moral actions and emotions in accord with reason, and virtuous states of character. Ultimately, then, Aquinas understands our good to involve right behavior, proper character, and appropriate emotional responses, and this view is hardly overly intellectual in its approach to what is good for human beings.

One weakness in this account I note only in passing. To love someone requires not only willing what is objectively good for that person but also willing what that person desires or wants most deeply (at least when this does not conflict with what is objectively good). Aquinas's account of what it is to will good for a person is simply not personal enough.

Let us leave this point behind and move on, however, for, according to Aquinas, to love someone is not only to will good for that individual but also to recognize that person as good. In order to complete our understanding of Aquinas's view of God's love for us, we must ask what God recognizes to be good about us. There is a simple answer here and a complicated one as well. The simple answer is that God recognizes our being to be good, for Aquinas thinks that insofar as anything exists, it has goodness. This response, of course, does not compel one to deny that some persons are evil. All it requires is that things are good in some sense solely by virtue of the fact that they exist. This goodness that results from existence can be outweighed or overridden by corruption of character so that a person turns out on the whole to be evil.

The complicated answer to the question concerns the ground that Aquinas posits for the simple answer. He is not content merely to assert that God recognizes our existence to be good. Instead, he wishes to construct a moral theory that explains why this is so. According to that theory, our being is recognized as good because the term 'goodness' and the term 'being' refer to the same thing.[23] Both terms refer to being, although in different senses. 'Being' refers to being with the sense of something's being actual or existent; 'goodness' refers to being also, but under the description and with the sense of something's being desirable. For Aquinas, what is desirable is the actualization of the capacity specific to the kind of thing in question. When the kind in question is humanity, the capacity specific to that kind of thing is rationality. The goodness of humans is tied specifically to the fulfillment of their rational nature. Thus, the ordinary sense of 'being' refers to a thing's actual existence, whereas the ordinary sense of 'goodness' refers to the fulfillment of the thing's nature, which is brought about by the actualization of its specific capacity. As the capacity is actualized, something is brought into being that did not exist before, that is, something that existed only potentially comes to have actual being. Thus, by the actualization of a capacity, being is increased. In essence, then, to behave poorly would be to aim at a decrease of being, and for God to love us is for him to aim at an increase of being.

The important point for our purposes is not the complicated

defense of the view but the view itself: What God recognizes as good in us is simply our existence or being. According to Stump, this fact has important implications for our understanding of hell, for in order for hell to issue out of God's love for humanity, it is necessary that it be the best way open to God to aim at an increase of being. Because to love God and hence participate in the union with God that is heaven is to will freely only what is in accord with God's will, God cannot ensure by his actions alone that all will be saved. The question then arises what God is to do with those who will not be saved. Such persons will not will what is necessary in order to participate in heaven, so such persons must be consigned to some kind of eternal existence separate from God in some sense, or God must annihilate such persons. Stump argues for the first of these alternatives:

> Should he [God] then annihilate them? To annihilate them is to eradicate their being; but to eradicate being on Aquinas's theory is a prima facie evil, which an essentially good God could not do unless there were an overriding good which justified it. Given Aquinas's identification of being and goodness, such an overriding good would have to produce or promote being in some way, but it is hard to see how the wholesale annihilation of persons could produce or promote being. In the absence of such an overriding good, however, the annihilation of the damned is not morally justified and thus not an option for a good God. On Aquinas's account, then, it is not open to God either to fulfill the natures of such persons or to eradicate them.[24]

Stump then outlines Dante's view of hell. His view provides a middle ground between heaven and annihilation for the damned. What God does is treat such persons so as to maximize the goodness of their acquired nature. He consigns them to a place where they cannot harm the innocent and thereby shows concern for their being by providing an environment that prevents the further "disintegration" of their being. Thereby he shows love for the being they have.

Stump's account of hell is importantly different from the strong view of hell and simple alternatives to it. She rejects all these views by denying both the No Escape Thesis and the Retribution Thesis. As noted earlier, she holds a quarantine model of hell, and she holds, not that no one can get out of hell, but that as a matter of fact no one ever does.[25] However, her rejection of the strong view and simple alternatives to it does not fully explain the power of her view of hell. Instead, its strength is found in the fact that it is an issuant conception of hell. Stump explains how hell flows from the very characteristics of God from which heaven flows. Her view is compatible with—even takes advantage of—the fact that God's fundamental characteristic in relation to human beings is love. Thus in Stump's view the claim of the inscription over Dante's hell is maintained: Hell was built by divine power, by the highest wisdom, and by primordial love.

Despite its virtues, however, this view of hell cannot be maintained. I focus on two problems here. The first concerns the relationship between the quarantine conception of hell and the moral principle that being ought to be enhanced. The second problem concerns the role that freedom plays in this account.

On Stump's account of hell, in order to aim at the preservation or enhancement of the being of those who will not be saved, God is supposed to preserve the being they have (i.e., the degree to which their behavior is rational and hence moral) by isolating them so that no one is affected by their actions, or at least no one who does not deserve it in the first place. The difficulty here is whether quarantining is adequate to the task set for it. First, note that the second option, according to which God quarantines those who refuse to be saved so that they harm only those who deserve to be harmed, will not work. The difficulty is that it is not a sufficient justification for X to harm Y by doing A that Y deserves to have A done to Y. It is also necessary, in order for the punishment to conform to the demands of pure justice, that X be a legitimate "dispenser of justice" and that X do A to Y *for the purposes of justice.* God could decree that X is a legitimate dispenser of justice, but X is going to have to cooperate if the punishment is to be done for the sake of justice. Hence, God will not have succeeded in preserving whatever degree of moral character X has by isolating, for example, bullies with those who deserve to be bullied. In spite of the fact that Y deserves to be bullied, X's character will deteriorate even further unless X bullies Y for the sake of justice. More generally, it does not justify the harm inflicted on Y that Y deserves it. Justifying the harm done in this way presupposes that X is doing A to Y with some intention relevant to justice, perhaps doing A to Y in order to secure some reform in Y, or in order to better society, or in order to punish Y,[26] and this presupposition need not be true. Thus it is not clear at all that God would preserve the being of a sinner by quarantining that person only with those who deserve to be affected by the consequences of whatever particular proclivities that sinner displays.

Stump might reply that, to continue the example, once full bullyhood has been reached, no further deterioration of being will result from further acts of unwarranted bullying. However, that is unlikely. Bullying can be done in a variety of ways, as is true of many other instances of wrongdoing, ways that involve other kinds of wrongdoing beyond the bullying itself. Furthermore, human beings generally become bored by repeated patterns, so we have no guarantee that bullies would not endeavor to bully creatively, so to speak, thereby contributing to further deterioration of being. In sum, quarantining simply provides no guarantee that deterioration will cease.

Note that this problem occurs not only in the third-person case, where one person is wronging another, but also in the first-person case, where one wrongs oneself in thought or deed. In any case of wrongdoing, one not only wrongs God and other persons but also wrongs oneself by contributing to a lower kind of moral character, a lower kind of existence, than what ought to be. In order, then, to preserve the being an individual has from further disintegration, God would have to prevent a person from doing any wrong whatsoever. Doing so, however, would obviously eliminate the freedom of the person in question, and hence is incompatible with the position of Aquinas and Stump.

The obvious solution to these problems is to attempt to restate the moral principle on which the view of hell depends. So, instead of claiming that God should act to preserve whatever degree of being a sinner has, perhaps the fundamental moral obligation should be thought of as involving the preservation or enhancement of being *to the degree possible*. In that case, perhaps, the quarantine model explains how God does the best he can to preserve the being of those who ultimately reject him. The best that can be done is to slow the "disintegration" of being rather than actually stop it. By doing so, God would neither interfere with the freedom of any individual nor annihilate anyone.

For the moment, let us grant that this response is acceptable. We shall return to it later, but before doing so, we need to turn to the second issue, which concerns the place of freedom in the Thomistic moral theory on which Stump's view of hell depends. In particular, the issue of the status of freedom in Aquinas's moral theory relates to the issue between those who hold an annihilationist understanding of hell and those who do not, that is, between those who deny and those who affirm the Existence Thesis of the strong view of hell. As Stump argues, if being is the fundamental value, justifying annihilation is difficult. However, if freedom is of fundamental value, annihilation seems to be easier to justify. First, it might be justified if the person in question chose annihilation over its alternatives, not in any indirect way but by directly intending his or her own destruction.[27] In addition, annihilation may even be justified in cases of indirect choice—cases where something is directly intended, which implies annihilation. One way to intend such a thing is to intend to achieve separation from the presence and blessings of God. Annihilation might be justified in such a case if the person is aware of the implications of this intention. (Because traditional theism ascribes omnipresence to God, intending separation from him implies annihilation in that there is no place God is not.)

So important considerations are at stake in determining the place of freedom in Aquinas's moral theory. First, freedom clearly plays a critical role in this conception, for it is part of the account of why God cannot redeem all persons. Further, there is a line of argument suggesting that freedom cannot be secondary in importance to being. The argument claims that, in order to explain the falsity of necessary universalism, freedom must be at least equal in importance to being, for if freedom is important but being is more important, God should sacrifice the importance of freedom in order to complete the being of any person bent on rejecting him.[28] So, the argument goes, if freedom is less important than being, Stump's view of hell will be incapable of explaining the falsity of necessary universalism. Hence, it must be concluded that freedom is not less important than being.

We have the appearance of a problem here, because the moral principle Stump elicits from Aquinas claims that the enhancement of being is the one thing at which to aim. The points made so far leave open the possibility, however, that the difficulty is only apparent. To see how, recall that Aquinas's conception is that to love us God must treat us according to our nature. Because the nature in question is rationality, perhaps freedom is inviolable, not because it is a fundamental moral value, but rather because it is an essential component of our rational natures. On this option, only being is the fundamental moral value, but its fundamental importance implies that freedom is inviolable. To aim at the well-being of humans, one must aim at the realization of the potential of humanity for rationality. Because freedom is an essential constituent of rationality, one could not aim at the well-being of humans without honoring their freedom.

This explanation does provide a solution to the question of the relationship between the importance of being and the importance of freedom. It creates another difficulty, however, in the context of our earlier conclusion that the moral principle to follow is not to preserve being but rather to hinder disintegration as much as possible when preservation and enhancement of being are not possible. This conclusion arose when we noted that disintegration of being may be something God cannot prevent in those who ultimately reject him. The question we must ask concerns the logical end of an eternal process of disintegration. Because our good is, for Aquinas, tied directly to our capacity for rationality, the logical end of an eternal process of disintegration would seem to be the loss of our capacity for rationality. Furthermore, if the end of this process is the loss of the capacity for rationality, according to the previous position about the relationship between the importance of freedom and being, the end of the process is a loss of the capacity for freedom as well. If the logical end of the process of disintegration is the loss of freedom, however, this view of hell has no response to the universalists' claims that freedom ought to be overridden to secure the presence of everyone in heaven. Freedom is lost either way, and it is certainly better lost in the interests of presence in heaven than in such a way that presence in hell is secured.[29]

The conclusion to be drawn here is that there is some tension between the moral theory, with its emphasis on the fundamental importance of being, and the quarantine model of hell. The moral theory has no capacity to explain why seclusion in hell is morally preferable to forced residence in heaven when the logical end of seclusion in hell is the loss of freedom. Yet Stump holds, rightly I think, that forced residence in heaven is not justified or desirable. Hence, if the moral theory in question is to explain why God does not force residence in heaven on those who try to reject him, it will have to do so at the cost of rejecting the quarantine model of hell.

Giving up the quarantine model of hell does not require affirming the annihilation view of hell, however. One might still think that some eternal existence picture of hell is to be preferred over any annihilation view on the basis of the moral principle involved in Aquinas's moral theory. However, this principle is controversial. Cases of rational suicide reveal deep problems with such a view.[30] As I have already argued in response to an argument of Talbott's, in some such cases, interference is unwarranted. Now, how can this be, if our fundamental obligation is to aim at an increase of being? Obviously, failure to interfere, although warranted, allows a decrease of being on Aquinas's account. Hence, there is reason to think that the argument against the annihilation position depending on Aquinas's moral principle fails.

These remarks do not imply that the annihilation position is correct, for difficult and complicated matters have yet to be addressed here (we turn to them in the next chapter). The only point I am arguing for here is that we cannot account for the importance of rationality and the accompanying importance of freedom by claiming that its importance is implied by our fundamental moral obligation to increase being.

Conclusion

We have seen that an adequate doctrine of hell must be an issuant conception of hell, and we have seen two accounts of hell that satisfy this constraint. Unfortunately, neither is adequate. Interestingly, both face the same problem of how to avoid an annihilation view of hell. The value of these accounts, however, is not found in their ability to withstand objection, but rather as examples of what an adequate account of hell must look like. Their inadequacies are also instructive, for the rock on which they founder—whether hell involves annihilation and the corollary issue concerning whether being or something involving freedom is of ultimate value—is the cornerstone issue for an adequate account of hell. On the one hand, there are the objective facts about what is in the person's best interests, which involves union with God, according to Christianity. If freedom were not very important and if the capacity for self-determination were a minor subplot in the interactions between God and humanity, God would do right to override our freedom and ensure the presence of all in heaven. We have already seen and rejected Talbott's argument for this view, so we cannot now conclude that freedom and the capacity for self-determination are of little significance. That some persons seek to avoid the union with God involved in heavenly existence is at least possible. What remains, then, is the task of giving an account of the nature of hell, and here the role played by the capacity for self-determination will be crucial. Once one recognizes the importance of the capacity for self-determination, one might well wonder whether choosing annihilation for oneself is possible and whether such a choice would need to be honored by God. Thus in developing such an account in the next chapter, a fundamental question will be, What is the relationship between the importance of the capacity for self-determination and the importance of existence itself?

Notes

1. Marilyn Adams, "Divine Justice, Divine Love, and the Life to Come," *Crux* 13 (1976–1977): 12–28.

2. Thomas P. Talbott, "The Doctrine of Everlasting Punishment," *Faith and Philosophy* 7.1 (January 1990): 19–43.

3. Augustine, *Enchiridion*, xxv.

4. Aquinas, *Summa Theologica*, I, Q. 23, Article 3.

5. Peter Geach, *Providence and Evil* (Cambridge, 1977), p. 147.

6. Talbott, "Everlasting Punishment," p. 22.

7. Ibid., pp. 23–30.

8. Perhaps what the strong view assumes is that there are only two relevant characteristics in the interaction between God and humanity so that, once God's love has been rejected, all that remains is for the interaction to be based on God's justice. Some of the problems with this assumption are obvious and have been discussed elsewhere to such an extent that a reminder of the difficulties would amount to mere repetition. However, one problem has not been raised as yet: The first part of the assumption—that there are only two relevant characteristics in the interaction between God and humanity—needs some defense as well as the latter part. Such a defense must generate a requirement of intimacy between God and humanity in order to rule out the option that he simply ignore us and let us go our own way, and perhaps the doctrine of conservation can be employed here to provide a ground of this intimacy requirement. Apart from this particular defense, all that remains, as far as I can tell, is to make God's role as the moral judge of the universe primary, thereby relegating his love to a secondary role in God's interaction with humanity. This latter option is not a propitious one, for although God's role as moral judge should not be abandoned we should not be happy with an account of God's interactions with humanity that relegates his love to a secondary role.

9. Spoken at the Colloquy of Montbelliard in 1586, quoted by Pierre Bayle, *Oeuvres Diverses*, T. III (La Haye, 1727), p. 814, and Gottfried Wilhelm Leibniz, *Essais de théodicée sur la bonté de Dieu, la liberté de l'homme, et origene du mal* (Amsterdam, 1734), Pt. II, p. 126.

10. Pierre Jurieu, *Apologie pour les Réformateurs* (Rotterdam, 1683), quoted from D. P. Walker, *The Decline of Hell* (Chicago, 1964), pp. 199–200.

11. For a defense of this claim, see Thomas V. Morris and Christopher Menzel, "Absolute Creation," *American Philosophical Quarterly* 23 (1986): 353–362.

12. If some version of a divine command theory is adequate, we may be under the demands of morality in another way in which God is not. The commands of God may underlie morality, or a great portion of it. Because holding that God's commands have a metaphysical status higher than he has would be unusual, morality would have a status above us but not above God. For a recent discussion of the prospects for a divine command theory, see Philip Quinn, "The Recent Revival of Divine Command Ethics," *Philosophy and Phenomenological Research*, vol. 50 supplement (Fall 1990): 345–366.

13. For a more complete discussion of this view of divine goodness and

its connection to praiseworthiness, see Thomas V. Morris, "Duty and Divine Goodness," *American Philosophical Quarterly* 21 (1984): 261–268, reprinted in Morris's *Anselmian Explorations* (Notre Dame, 1987), pp. 26–41.

14. Malebranche, *Entretiens sur la Métaphysique et sur la religion* (1688), quoted from Walker, *The Decline of Hell*, p. 207.

15. Ibid., pp. 109–110.

16. C. S. Lewis, *The Problem of Pain* (New York, 1973), p. 111.

17. Ibid., pp. 113–114.

18. Ibid., p. 113.

19. Ibid. pp. 114–115.

20. Eleonore Stump, "Dante's Hell, Aquinas's Moral Theory, and the Love of God," *Canadian Journal of Philosophy* 16 (1986): 181–198.

21. Ibid., p. 191.

22. Ibid.

23. Although this claim is indeed a surprising one, it has been excellently defended recently in Eleonore Stump and Norman Kretzmann, "Being and Goodness," in *Divine and Human Action: Essays in the Metaphysics of Theism*, ed. Thomas V. Morris (Ithaca, N.Y. 1988), pp. 281–312.

24. Stump, "Dante's Hell," p. 196.

25. Ibid., p. 198.

26. Such an assumption is ordinarily made regarding our own penal system. Once one devotes even minimal thought to the assumption, the justice of our penal system is suspect indeed; but, then again, perhaps this is the best we could hope for in terms of approaching ideal justice.

27. We shall see later that certain restrictions must be applied to the circumstances of the choice for annihilation to be justified, but the point remains that some choices for annihilation may need to be honored if freedom is the fundamental moral value.

28. Talbott's argument is instructive here, for our earlier rejection of it requires that the importance of freedom not be overridden by the value of having no one end up in hell.

29. Stump might respond that freedom is essential to, but not an essential component of, rationality. If so, the loss of rationality would not entail the loss of freedom. If one were to attempt to rescue Aquinas's theory in this way from the problem in the text, however, one is left with no explanation of why God allows freedom to be used in such a way that the destruction of rationality occurs. That straightforwardly implies that freedom is more important than being, given Aquinas's other claims.

30. A defender of Aquinas might reply that there cannot be any cases of rational suicide by claiming that a rational action is a moral one and there are no morally justified cases of suicide. The proper reply is that the theory of rationality here is mistaken. There may be some specifiable sense of 'rational' on which a rational action is a moral one, but there are other senses in which a rational action need not be a moral one. All that is needed for the present argument is the claim that there is some sense of 'rational'

such that, when an action is rational in this sense, interference by others is not warranted. Suicides in the face of immense suffering are just of this sort, and if a moral theorist wishes to insist that the action is morally wrong, we need not disagree to make the point that interference with the action is unjustified.

4

Freedom, Existence, and the Nature of Hell

Our investigation of the problem of hell has yielded several important conclusions to this point, a summary of which may be useful before proceeding further. First, we have seen the failure of the traditional conception of hell and standard alternatives to it. Furthermore, the way in which the standard alternatives are defective sheds light on our subject, for they fare no better than the traditional conception in avoiding difficulty; in fact, we can fairly say that many of these alternatives, formed in the face of perceived inadequacies of the traditional view, fail to make any substantial progress at all toward solving the problem of hell. This result is singularly important in the present context, for it serves to demonstrate the fact that the problem of hell is not limited in scope to varieties of traditional Christianity. Whether the proffered alternative is a version of universalism, annihilationism, or conditional immortalism, or a second chance doctrine, no such view, offered as a simple alternative to the traditional doctrine of hell, can solve the problem of hell. So the problems with the traditional conception and simple alternatives to it show that the problem of hell is not easily solved. The standard view of the matter is that either the objections to the strong view can be answered or, if they cannot, a variety of alternatives to the strong view are available to solve the problem. So, the line goes, if the strong view is inadequate, the task is to sort out the best among a host of adequate views. This view of the matter is deeply misleading, and it has been the point of the last several chapters to show that this account of the matter is naive. The results of the first two chapters show the need for a more comprehensive approach to the problem of hell, as opposed to the limited approach to the problem that arises from dropping certain aspects of the traditional conception of hell to yield a simple alternative to it. This comprehensive approach was begun in the last chapter, where I argued that our understanding of hell must be rooted in an acceptable portrayal of the character of God. I also argued that the portrayal of God's character that Christians should accept makes God's love his primary motivational characteristic. Of course, Christians should also hold that God is just as well as loving, for if he were not just, he could not be perfectly good. However, the point of holding that love is God's primary motivational characteristic implies that the demands of his justice never arise apart from considerations of his love for the created order, and hence no account of hell that appeals only to God's justice in explaining hell can offer a fully comprehensive solution to the problem of hell. As I have been putting it, an adequate conception of hell must be an issuant conception of it, one that portrays hell as flowing from the same divine character from which heaven flows. Any other view wreaks havoc on the integrity of God's character.

Once one becomes comfortable with this perspective, the fundamental flaw of the traditional conception of hell and the standard alternatives is easy to appreciate. All such views rely intrinsically on a retributive punishment model of hell. For instance, both the traditional conception and annihilationism (and conditional immortalism) construe hell fundamentally as a place of punishment; they merely disagree about the Existence Thesis. They disagree, that is, about the kind of punishment hell involves. Perhaps more surprising is the way in which second chance doctrines and universalism rely on the very same model. Each takes hell to be fundamentally a place of punishment, and each attempts to find some way to avoid the problems that arise once one accepts this feature. Second chance doctrines offer an afterlife possibility of escape, and universalists claim that no one will actually undergo such treatment because all will be saved. Once we take note of the fact that an adequate conception of hell must be an issuant conception of it, it is not surprising that each of these views of hell is deeply problematic. The way they all retain the retributive punishment model of hell explains why each such view is subject to the particular defects uncovered in the first two chapters.

My claim that the retributive punishment model is defective should not be taken to imply that hell does not involve punishment. The point is rather that our fundamental conception of hell cannot be in terms of the concepts of justice or desert. How exactly we are to conceive it we began to address in the last chapter and is part of the point of the present chapter, but even without an adequate alternative at this point we can note the failure of the retributive punishment model. What I have been suggesting over the course of this book is that this punishment model lies at the heart of the usual approaches to the problem of hell, for the affirmation of this model by the traditional conception of hell and the standard alternatives to it explains the inadequacy of their attempts to solve the problem of hell. Moreover, I have also been arguing that any hope for success in addressing the problem of hell rests on jettisoning this usual approach to the problem.

In the last chapter, we began to work toward the goal of finding a conception of hell to meet the problems we have encountered. To that end, we examined the views of Lewis and Stump because each offers an account of hell that is not a simple alternative to the strong view and does not rely on the punishment model. In each case, however, problems remain. The point of the present chapter is to take up the issues that remain to see what an adequate conception of hell must be like.

The immediate pressing question that must be addressed to provide a complete account of hell concerns those goods the residents of heaven enjoy and of which the rest are deprived. The conclusion of the last chapter suggested two possibilities. One is that the fundamental good lacking in hell is the heavenly community, in which eternal bliss is found in union with God and with others freed from the imperfections of the human condition. This suggestion yields a privative picture of the pain of hell, for it accounts for the evil of hell in terms of what it lacks compared to heaven. In this view, those in hell are exiled from heaven because they are not fit for it, and for this reason I call this view 'the exile doctrine of hell'. The second possibility is that the fundamental good lacking in hell is not only the blessings of the heavenly community but existence itself. We can call this account 'the annihilation doctrine of hell'.[1]

As we saw in the last chapter, the primary issue between these two doctrines is whether freedom or existence is of fundamental moral importance. Aquinas's position was that existence is the primary value; however, we found no way to reconcile this claim with the emphasis placed on freedom in Aquinas's position. Hence, we must undertake the project apart from the intricacies of his theory.

Our best understanding of the issue of the relative importance of existence compared to freedom arises by considering analogues in human experience of the afterlife alternatives of exile and annihilation. These analogues are capital punishment and suicide, and each pulls us in a different direction on the issue of the importance of being and freedom. On the one hand, penal considerations favor thinking that existence is more important than freedom. Whether one believes capital punishment is justified, it is worse (even if justified) than life imprisonment. So if some choose separation from God and the heavenly community, penal considerations might favor a self-chosen exile doctrine over the annihilation doctrine. On the other hand, paternalism issues in suicide cases seem to lead us in the other direction. The choice to commit suicide can be a rational choice in some circumstances (I will have more to say about this possibility later), and the self-conscious choice of the depraved to be separate from God might be the same kind of choice as a choice for suicide. One may know that because God is omnipresent, there is no place where God is not, and one may also be so warped by one's opposition to God that anything (even nonexistence itself) is conceived to be preferable to remaining in the presence of God. Such a person would desire annihilation. Suppose that this desire is a rational one, just as the choice for suicide in the earthly life might be rational. If so, it might seem unduly paternalistic for God to continue to sustain such a person. Hence, considerations surrounding the possibility of rational suicide may seem to suggest that, no matter how important existence is, intervention is sometimes too paternalistic to be justified, and hence the importance of freedom wins out over the importance of existence. If so, however, it would seem that the annihilation doctrine is to be preferred to the exile doctrine.

The first task of this chapter—addressing the question of the importance of existence compared to freedom—requires an investigation of these conflicting thoughts. I first examine the import of considerations concerning the nature of capital punishment and then the competing considerations about suicide. After examining these considerations, we shall be able to reach a conclusion about the issue of the relative importance of freedom and existence.

Incarceration

The issue before us is the status of the penal argument for the exile doctrine. According to it, the annihilation doctrine would be preferable to the exile doctrine only if capital punishment were less severe than life imprisonment; because capital punishment is obviously the more severe of the two, the exile doctrine is to be preferred.

Things are not quite that simple, however. First, it is true not only that death is objectively a bad thing but also that most conceive death to be a bad thing as well. Under these circumstances, obviously the death penalty is a worse kind of punishment than life imprisonment. What is not clear, however, is whether it is the objective feature of the intrinsic evil of death or the subjective feature of the person's conceiving of death as bad that plays the most significant role in explaining which kind of punishment is worse. In particular, if the emphasis is placed on the second, subjective consideration, it is no longer clear that capital punishment is intrinsically worse than life imprisonment. If only the subjective consideration counts, then if a person wanted to die or thought death preferable, life imprisonment might be worse.

Second, life in our prison system is not devoid of all that is good and rewarding in life. The more devoid incarceration is of that which is good and rewarding in life, the less clear it is that incarceration is a less severe form of punishment than the death penalty. If, for example, life in prison was constituted by solitary confinement in a cell permitting no movement and subject to no lighting source of any sort, it would no longer be clear that life imprisonment is morally preferable to capital punishment.

The penal argument for the exile view is therefore not conclusive. It would be conclusive only if the purely objective features of the incarcerative situation explained why capital punishment is rightly thought to be a worse punishment than life imprisonment. It is far from clear, however, that our moral evaluation here owes only to purely objective factors. Most important, it seems likely that part of what accounts for our judgment that the death penalty is more severe than life imprisonment is that the ordinary kinds of prisons do not eliminate all that makes life subjectively worthwhile. When all such features are removed, that life in prison is preferable to death no longer is clear. Hence, the penal argument for the exile doctrine fails.

Suicide and the Argument from Rational Suicide

Consider, then, the suicide argument for the annihilation doctrine. According to it, the annihilation doctrine should be favored because we would be overly paternalistic and hence wrong to interfere in some suicide attempts. In order to evaluate the force of this argument, let us begin by dividing cases of suicide into two kinds: those involving impending death and those not involving impending death. In our own time, the issues involved in the latter sort of suicide are crystallized in existential philosophy, burdened as it is with the question of whether to end one's meaningless existence. Can we learn anything for our project from their predicament?

There are problems in attempting to extend anything we might learn about the nature of hell from considering such cases of suicide. If we are to trust the word of existentialists, the existentialist predicament arises from a conviction that God does not exist, and no such predicament need arise in the afterlife.[2] If they are mistaken in their understanding of what makes life worth living, their thinking about the issue of suicide cannot help us, for no argument for the annihilation doctrine ought to hinge on the confusion of those making a suicidal choice. Alternatively, if they have adequately diagnosed the meaning of life, the assumption of this work is that they are mistaken about whether there is a God, and hence, once again, their thoughts on the matter are irrelevant. So, in either case, no existentialist considerations regarding suicide give us any clue as to whether the suicide argument for the annihilation doctrine is adequate.

We turn, then, to the other kind of suicide, suicide in the face of impending death. Some such suicides are both irrational and morally impermissible, and such cases need not detain us. The other cases are much more instructive, however. Some such suicides are rational because of the close proximity of death and the route to it that lies ahead. When a person faces a significantly painful and protracted end to his or her life, a suicide may be rational, and no one else may be justified in interfering.

Applied to our issue concerning the afterlife, a defender of the annihilation doctrine can claim that a person in the afterlife can be so warped psychologically and morally that existence with God is thought of in terms of (and perhaps would be experienced as) suffering. The envisioned suffering would be unending and thus would differ from the case of rational suicide in the face of protracted suffering. Nevertheless, this difference is not crucial. In the mind of the sufferer, it is not the fact of death at the end of suffering that warrants committing suicide, it is rather the suffering itself (with no hope of things getting better) that is the critical feature of the situation. Were such suffering unending rather than issuing in death, the alternatives would not seem significantly different to the sufferer. From a subjective point of view, the alternatives would still be as they are now—end it all right now, or face the insufferable.

Thus a strong argument would seem available on behalf of the annihilation doctrine, an argument proceeding from the possibility of rational suicides in the face of permanent suffering. The argument, in essence, proceeds as follows. It first claims that there are suicides that are rational. Some such suicides are by persons who conceive of the alternatives as suicide versus some state of affairs conceived to be intolerable (and this conception is not the result of insanity or some other sort of mental deficiency of the person in question). In such cases, people ought to be allowed the option they choose; hence, if in the afterlife an analogous situation arises, annihilation ought to be an option as well.

The argument here hinges on a connection between freedom and unachievable objects of desire. Because these goods are unachievable, some will view their situation as intolerable and choose suicide. The argument then attempts to draw an inference to the annihilation doctrine, but the argument remains a bit mysterious because there are a number of interpretations of the notion of a good being unachievable on which it depends. Two that immediately come to mind are the objective and subjective interpretations. An objective interpretation takes the description to refer to goods that *are in fact unachievable*, and on this interpretation the argument relies on the moral principle that if the most significant goods for a person *are in fact unachievable*, his or her freedom to bring an end to existence ought not to be subject to interference. A different interpretation is a subjective one. It takes the description to refer to goods that *are thought to be unachievable*. On this interpretation, the argument relies on the subjective moral principle that claims that if the most significant goods for that person *are thought to be unachievable*, that person should be free to choose nonexistence.

Neither of these principles is adequate, however. The objective principle does not support the annihilation doctrine, for nothing in the account of hell as developed to this point implies that the most significant goods for a person are unachievable in the afterlife. For this implication to hold, some version of the No Escape Thesis would have to be included in the description of hell. No such thesis is a part of the theory to this point, so there is no reason yet to hold that what is objectively good for a person is in fact unachievable in the afterlife.

In addition, reflection on justified interventions in suicide attempts suggests that it is not objective considerations that justify intervention. The moral claim underlying the objective principle is that objective considerations explain when intervention is justified and when it is not, but this claim is mistaken. When a person is confused or depressed, thinking that all is hopeless, intervention is justified because the person will be grateful for the intervention once no longer depressed or confused. Part of what is required to treat other agents as autonomous is sometimes to allow them to make their own choices, even when those choices are bad.

I am not denying that there can be reasons to override this autonomy consideration. We might override it for other moral reasons, such as the needs of the person's dependents. The state might also have an interest in fostering intervention even in such cases because of its interest in the continued existence of its citizens. My use of moral terms such as 'right', 'wrong', 'obligation', 'permission', and the like leaves open the possibility of these terms applying but being overridden by further factors. My point is that we lose sight of an important moral feature if we do not see that it takes overriding considerations to justify intervention when it is known that the person in question will not come to agree with that intervention. So the moral claim underlying the objective principle is false, and hence the objective principle does not appeal to those features of the case that are relevant from the moral point of view. Hence, no argument depending on that principle ought to be used to undergird the annihilation doctrine of hell.

The subjective principle is inadequate as well, for it is too weak. Many times people think their prospects are hopeless when suicide prevention is fully appropriate. For one thing, some persons are given to feelings of hopelessness at the slightest provocation, and to allow such individuals to commit suicide would be heartless. Other times, the despair a person experiences is only fleeting, and intervention is appropriate because that person will "see things differently in the morning."

So a different principle is required for the argument for the annihilation doctrine. For that argument, we need a principle midway between the subjective and objective principles described here, one that honors the subjective features required to warrant intervention but that is not overly subjective in the way the subjective principle is. We can begin to make some progress on this front by qualifying the subjective principle. One necessary qualification is that the thoughts and beliefs about the unachievability of the good must be rational ones. With this qualification, the principle reads: If the most significant goods for that person (i.e., those goods judged to be essential for a continued life to be worthwhile) *are rationally thought to be unachievable,* that person should be free to choose nonexistence. I will call this principle "the rationality principle."

There is a strong temptation here to view the rationality principle as one that replaces the False with the Obscure, for the notion of rationality is notoriously vague and perhaps ambiguous. What is needed is a bit of detail about what notion of rationality would be appropriate in our setting. Our discussion to this point has shown that subjective features are essential to our topic, and some progress can be made in clarifying the kind of subjectivity needed by specifying an appropriately subjective sense of rationality. The sense I have in mind we might term "the egocentric sense" of rational belief. A belief or thought is egocentrically rational for S at time t just in case S would hold that belief or thought at t, were S to reflect on the truth of that belief or thought, being interested in the belief or thought only in terms of its truth or falsity, until no more reflection would alter the view S holds about that belief or thought.[3] This account is subjective in that it appeals to no standards of evidence or perspectives on the truth other than the individual's own. As such, it is appropriate to the issue of interference with the capacity for self-determination.

This understanding of the rationality principle goes some distance toward explaining why intervention is warranted in some suicide cases and not in others. It does not help us understand, however, the importance of the issue of what a person will feel like "in the morning." This egocentric understanding of rationality indexes the subjective features employed in the principle to particular times, and the issue of what a person will feel like in the morning is a cross-temporal issue. So in addition to requiring that the thoughts and beliefs are egocentrically rational, it is also important that they are rational in a settled—that is, cross-temporal—fashion. Let us say that a rational belief of S's that p is a settled rational belief of S's just in case it will always be rational for S to believe that p, and it is rational for S to believe that it will always be so. The rationality principle then gives way to a settled rationality principle, where the notion of rationality in question is understood to be egocentric rationality. The settled rationality principle claims that if a person has a settled egocentrically rational belief or thought that the most significant goods are unachievable, no one else is permitted to interfere with that person's choice of suicide.

This view has several advantages. First, it is not subject to the difficulties plaguing the subjective principle. For one thing, one's beliefs can be fleeting and ephemeral, formed in the presence of sudden mood swings and abandoned in the presence of opposite mood swings. Settled rational beliefs are not like that. Again, beliefs can be held that only the slightest reflection would reveal to be false;

egocentrically rational beliefs are quite different. This principle also avoids the difficulties of the objective principle. It does not require the truth of the No Escape Thesis for interference in the process of self-determination to be unwarranted. Even if the No Escape Thesis were false, a person could still rationally (although depravedly) believe that nonexistence is preferable to dependence on God.

One issue must still be addressed. It concerns the role of "interfering" factors regarding deliberation, factors such as physical pain and mental illness of various sorts. Suppose, for example, that a person in severe pain appears to have fully deliberated about ending his or her life and appears to have reached a settled conclusion that suicide is appropriate. Should we interfere in such a case if we believe that the decision is not dispassionate because of the severe pain? More generally, how should the presence of various interfering and even debilitating factors affect the decision to interfere?

These questions are answered by a full treatment of the notion of reflection that plays a part in the account of egocentric rationality. The issue concerns what kind of reflection we imagine a person engaging in when determining the truth of the matter. For example, many persons, upon reflecting for only a very short period of time, grow weary of reflection and abandon the project. When we are thinking of what is egocentrically rational for such a person to believe, do we imagine them reflecting, subject to such limiting predilections, or do we imagine them having a greater tolerance for reflective tasks? Again, suppose we are wondering whether it is reasonable for a certain person, suffering from a migraine headache, to believe certain things. Do we imagine the person reflecting while still suffering from the migraine, or do we imagine that person reflecting while unburdened by such discomfort?

These questions touch on an important and neglected issue, the issue of idealization in epistemology. When we ask whether a belief is rational, or justified, or counts as knowledge, we often idealize away from certain human limitations in arriving at an answer. For example, certain theories of rationality that emphasize conforming to the probability calculus idealize human rationality in such a way that it includes logical omniscience; that is, they hold humans rationally responsible for believing all the logical consequences of any of their beliefs. On the minimalist side of the idealization issue—the side opposing idealizations of any sort—is a theory that wants to describe what is rational for you to believe, given only actual facts about you, that is, given what (possibly flawed) views you hold about evidence, what you actually thought of and remembered from prior experience, and the like. This minimalist approach is unabashedly realistic about the epistemic agents for which it provides a theory of rationality. On the other end of the spectrum is a completely idealized theory of rationality, one we might call the God's-eye theory of rationality. According to it, we should idealize away from any practical limitations whatsoever, counting as rational a belief for a person that the person would believe if that person had a full understanding of the theory of evidence and a full grasp of the facts. Such a theory, of course, eliminates the distinction between a true belief and a rational one, and, as such, this sort of idealization is surely to be rejected.

More circumspect idealizations can be delimited by dividing off the theory of evidence from awareness of relevant data. On one such theory, we posit full acceptance of a complete theory of evidence, together with a fully realistic—that is, unidealized—picture of the data available to an individual at a time, data that function (together with the theory of evidence) to determine whether a belief is rational; that is, we idealize the theory of evidence completely, but do not idealize at all when it comes to what evidence a person has (e.g., if the person does not recall a piece of information, it cannot be relevant to what it is rational to believe). Alternatively, we might reverse things. We might idealize to full awareness of relevant data, but be fully realistic about the theory of evidence. There are also intermediate positions on the degree of idealization tolerable. For example, partial idealization regarding relevant data would result if we wish to count things one should have remembered at the time even if one did not in fact remember them, or if we wish to count present information one should have acquired even if, in fact, one did not acquire that information. Others might wish to idealize in terms of the theory of evidence or the data available, in some sense, to the culture in which one lives.

The issue of idealization as it touches the notion of egocentric rationality concerns the character of the reflection in which we imagine a person engaging. Although a full and complete treatment of this issue would take us much beyond the scope of this work, some cursory remarks can help us address the issue we are facing. There is a distinction between the faculties or abilities a person has and the various factors that can interfere with these faculties or abilities. When we ask what is egocentrically rational for a person to believe, we should consider what view that person would come to on the basis of unhindered use of the mental abilities she or he has; that is, we should not idealize in such a way that we posit greater abilities

to reason, but we should idealize away from factors that would interfere with the use of the capacities the person actually has. So, when
considering what is egocentrically rational for a person to believe
who is suffering from a migraine headache, for example, we should
consider what view that person would come to if he or she reflected
while free from the headache. We idealize in this way about rationality, but not to the extent that we consider what view such a
person would come to if, say, he or she were significantly more
intelligent than is actually the case.

None of this implies that there are no borderline cases when we
cannot distinguish between a feature of a mental capacity and a
hindering factor regarding that capacity. For example, certain types
of temporary mental illness are clearly hindering factors rather than
intrinsic features of the way a person reasons, weighs evidence,
posits explanations, and the like. Yet that there is always a core
capacity regarding which any mental illness is only an interfering
factor is far from clear. The more permanent a mental condition,
especially when it is untreatable, the more inclined we are to think
that the illness is an intrinsic feature of the reasoning capacity rather
than a mere hindrance.

The account as presented to this point regarding interference in
cases of suicide implies that intervention is not warranted when
persons have settled, egocentrically rational beliefs that are suicidal.
The issue regarding conditions—such as severe pain, mental illness,
drug-induced illusions, and the like—that might make us uncomfortable with allowing suicide are handled by an adequate account of
the kind of reflection involved in having an egocentrically rational
belief.

This principle takes us a long way toward completing the philosophical core of an account of hell. Conceived in the starkest terms,
the alternative to presence in heaven is nothingness. To choose to be
dependent on God is to choose a path that results in presence in
heaven, and to choose independence from God is, ultimately, to
choose annihilation, for independence from God is not logically possible. Furthermore, as we have seen, granting such a choice can be
justified, so there is reason to reject the exile doctrine because it
depends on the view that the value of existence always overrides the
importance of freedom.

One might object here that those who choose against heaven
need not be wishing for ontological independence from God, but are
rather choosing only against submission to the will of God. Such

people may not care one whit whether they are ontologically dependent on God as long as they do not have to obey him. Generally people rebel only against submission to God and not to ontological dependence on him. This attitude strikes me as a confusion, however, for any involvement by God in the life of a person involves more than mere sustenance of being. To presume that one can have sustenance of being with no further involvement by God is to presume falsely. Ultimately, the aim of a loving and holy God would be to develop all people to the point where they truly enjoy the company of heaven. If that is so, however, the aim of God must be to get them all to see that their ultimate choice is heaven or annihilation; there is no middle position in which God can reasonably be asked to sustain our being and yet ignore our predilection toward corruption. So, as claimed in the preceding paragraph, the exile doctrine of hell must be rejected.

These conclusions, however, do not imply the annihilation doctrine. Instead, all we are warranted in claiming is that, in an adequate account of hell, the fundamental alternative to heaven is as the annihilation doctrine claims. Once a person comes to see things with perfect perspicacity, no choice is available to an individual except that which ends in union with God or the ultimate separation from him, which is annihilation. What does not follow, however, is that anyone recognizes the true nature of this choice, nor does it follow that if a person chooses the ultimate separation of annihilation, the choice is granted. We might describe the position achieved to this point by thinking of hell on analogy with physical systems. One question that plagues philosophers of science is whether every physical system in nature can be understood completely through mechanical description, or whether description in terms of the *telos* of the system is required as well. If we appropriate this terminology, the results we have achieved show that the teleological character of hell differs from its mechanical character. We have concluded that the teleological character of hell is properly described in terms of annihilation, but we cannot infer from this claim, as the annihilation doctrine of hell does, that the objective, substantial character of hell—that is, its mechanical character—is annihilation. As with many physical systems, a teleological (or functional) description of the system tells us little about implementation, and just so with the character of hell. The position achieved to this point informs us only as to the teleological character of hell conceived as a system, but nothing at all about implementation, that is, nothing at all about the mechanical character of hell. In the remainder of this chapter, I want to complete an account of hell by indicating what its mechanical, as opposed to teleological, character might be.

Mechanical and Teleological Conceptions of Hell

The teleological features of hell derive from the fundamental fact that there is nowhere God is not and nothing fundamentally independent of him. The choice of heaven or hell is not a choice of residence, as if one were picking between two new countries in which one might wish to reside. The choice of heaven or hell is rather a choice between ultimate union with God and ultimate independence from God. Choosing to aim against ultimate union with him is choosing ultimate independence from him, which is to choose nonexistence. One does not have available a "geographic" alternative to heaven; that is, one cannot pick some desert landscape alternative to the supposedly lusher, more luxuriant realm of heaven. There simply is no ultimate alternative to the two possibilities of dependence on God or independence from God. A person may not see these points clearly, and even an abstract recognition of them may not be reflected in particular judgments made at particular times, but it takes confusion to see things teleologically in terms other than either God or nothing.

There is no guarantee, however, that such confusion can be eliminated. As we noted earlier, the way in which one responds to experience by altering one's complete view of the world may involve some decision about what parts of the view to treat as the "hard core" and what other parts to treat as the "outer belt" that is subject to revision. If decisions are involved in this way in one's view of the world, perhaps God could do nothing to make sure a person understood the facts of the matter. In fact, perhaps God could do nothing to make sure that all persons in the afterlife are theists—a clear precondition for viewing the ultimate alternatives as either God or nothing. Perhaps for some individuals, atheism is so much a "hard core" view that even the experience of an afterlife would be interpreted to maintain atheistic views.

Beyond these possibilities involving cognitive confusion are those who might come to see the alternatives clearly. Even in such cases, for those who clearly understand that the choice is between God and nothingness and who would nonetheless choose nothingness, there remains the question of what God is to do with them. It is not obvious that others should always do their part to secure the object of any person's choices, nor is it obvious that, should some choose nonexistence over blessedness, God should grant them their wish. The teleological account of hell just presented does not require that God grant all wishes for eternal separation from himself. Instead, the argument for the annihilation doctrine requires only that persons be given what they choose when their choices are based on settled rational beliefs. In the case at hand, the person must rationally believe in a settled way that the most significant goods for that person are unavailable and that nonexistence would be preferable. Nevertheless, there is no obvious guarantee that rejecting God at any moment of time would guarantee that such a person has a rational belief of this sort. Moreover, if the person lacks such a rational belief, the question is still open as to what hell for such an individual would be like, that is, what mechanical implementation would be appropriate to attempt to yield an appropriate conception of the final teleological alternatives. God would have no cause to grant these people their choices, just as we need not stand idly by and watch a suicide occur when we know that the person is in the grips of only momentary despair. Hence, the conclusion to draw here is that annihilation presents only a teleological conception of hell, but what substantive conception is appropriate is left open at this point.

These considerations suggest that annihilation is the limiting case of what happens to those who refuse the company of heaven. To choose against heaven is to be headed for nonbeing. I address later the question of what the experience of being headed for nonbeing might be like, but first let us consider whether any could reach the limit. If annihilation is the limiting case, is it the sure end of those in hell? Or is annihilation better thought of as that toward which one is headed by choosing not to be in heaven, but a destination that one never achieves? I wish to consider two arguments for this latter view, that no one could ever achieve the limiting case of annihilation. I argue that there is no good reason for thinking that annihilation is only a limiting case that can never be achieved.

Two Arguments Against the Substantial Reality of Annihilation

The first argument rehashes in a new context a position encountered in chapter 1. According to this argument, in the case of annihilation, God has to *commit* a certain action; in the case of allowing a rational suicide, one only has to *omit* intervening. Moreover, it might be claimed, omissions are easier to justify than commissions. So even if omissions in cases of rational suicide are justified, commissions in the afterlife by God are not, and hence annihilation is not a possibility.

This argument fails because, given the doctrine of divine conservation as outlined and defended in chapter 1, there is no distinction to be drawn between commissions and omissions by God when the result is nonexistence. If the defense of that doctrine is adequate, it follows that nonexistence is the natural predilection of all created beings; in order for continued existence to obtain, God must intervene. Hence, the above use of the omission/commission distinction improperly construes the relationship between God and his creation. In the afterlife as elsewhere, continued existence is the result of God's commissions, not his omissions. Hence, if certain omissions are justified in the case of rational suicide, the analogous omission in the afterlife situation has as its immediate and direct consequence annihilation.

The doctrine of divine conservation is controversial, however, and, should it be found wanting, reconsideration would be needed of the position I am defending, that the teleological character of hell is not a mere limit that can never be achieved. This argument thus provides important issues for continued reflection concerning the implementation of hell, as opposed to its teleological structure.

The other argument against the substantial reality of annihilation arises from considering the limitations on our knowledge of what people rationally believe or do not believe. When deciding whether to interfere in an attempted suicide, we must make a judgment about whether interfering is right. Surely mistakes are possible here. Yet, the adage goes, one should always "err on the side of life." So intervention is warranted if there is but the slimmest chance that a judgment for nonintervention is mistaken.

Usually the problem of fallibility is conceived as being limited to the finite realm. God is usually understood as not subject to the possibility of error; he is omniscient and could not fail to be omniscient.[4] Some, however, have thought that there are special problems with God's knowledge of what free individuals will or might do in the future. If we are to address fully the issue of not only the teleological character of hell but also its implementation or mechanical character, we need to see what effect these concerns have on the doctrine of hell.

The connection to the doctrine of hell occurs concerning the notion of a settled rational belief to which my argument for the annihilation view appeals. To know that a person has a rational belief of the required sort, God would have to be able to know what a person would think under certain specified conditions. The issues involved in knowing the truth of counterfactuals of this sort are the same issues bound up with the issue of whether God can have foreknowledge of what free individuals will or might do,[5] and many philosophers deny that such foreknowledge is possible.[6] If so, however, God would have to choose between knowing the minds of those not in heaven and leaving them free. On the assumption that freedom is of crucial moral importance, God would have to limit his knowledge in the process of creating free beings.

I am not convinced by arguments for the incompatibility of foreknowledge and freedom. I will not defend the compatibility of the two here,[7] but a brief summary of how the two might be conceived to be compatible might prove helpful. On the account I favor, the way God knows what free individuals will do is by knowing what are called "counterfactuals of freedom." A counterfactual of freedom is a claim of the form 'if person S were in circumstances C, S would freely choose to do A'. I believe humans sometimes know truths of this form. For example, I know that if I were to place my five-year-old son in the kitchen with a bowl of ice cream in front of him, he would eat some of it. Examples of this sort are found in religious texts as well. In 1 Samuel 23, David has Abiathar the priest bring the ephod so that David might receive answers to his questions concerning what Saul and the citizens of Keilah would do with him if he stays in Keilah. David's questions are answered in terms of the truth of certain counterfactuals of freedom: If he were to stay in Keilah, Saul would beseige the city, and the men of Keilah would surrender David to Saul. If there are true counterfactuals of freedom, this argument, based on fallibility of knowledge of what free individuals will do, does not show that annihilation is only a limiting case that no one will ever suffer. The issue is controversial, however, and the point to note is how a view about the mechanical character of hell depends on it.

The Composite View and Theological Constraints

We have seen the failure of two issuant conceptions of hell. The first, the exile doctrine, attempts to demonstrate that the Existence Thesis is true and that annihilation is never suffered by anyone. As a general view about the moral weight to be assigned to existence as compared with freedom, this position fails because of the considerations involved in the argument from rational suicide. Moreover, one

cannot grant the possibility of rational suicide but defend an inter-
ventionist policy in all cases in the afterlife in which a person might
choose the ultimate separation from God of annihilation. So the
exile account of hell cannot withstand scrutiny. However, the annihilation doctrine fares no better, for even the success of the argument from rational suicide fails to show that hell is annihilation. As
we have seen, it shows only that the teleological character of hell is
annihilation. The issue still remains of the implementation of the
system having this teleological character, the mechanism by which
a person, upon choosing against God and the heavenly community,
moves toward annihilation. No argument is available that would
warrant the annihilation of such individuals, for the only instructive
argument about the afterlife we have found acceptable is the argument from rational suicide, which would countenance annihilation
only when one finds present settled rational beliefs. Hence, hell
could not be constituted as identical with annihilation. Instead, hell
is a composite system with a teleological component, which is annihilation, and a mechanical component, which involves continued
existence. Hell is an afterlife journey toward annihilation. It may
even be true that some never get to the end of the road toward
annihilation; it may be, that is, that some eternally exist in hell,
never coming to see the alternatives clearly or never changing their
opposition to the heavenly community, and yet never achieving rationality for those beliefs and desires.

This composite view of hell completes the philosophical investigation of the doctrine of hell. One further question about hell could
be pursued, concerning what the experience of hell would be like
prior to annihilation. However, my goal has not been a complete
account of hell, but rather an account that is philosophically satisfactory in solving the problem of hell. I submit that the composite
view defended here is of that sort. It solves the problem of hell
because it places the responsibility for ending up in hell squarely on
the shoulders of those who choose that option. In particular, as I
have developed the view, it implies that for God to do otherwise
than to consign such individuals to hell would impugn God's goodness. Hence, not only is hell compatible with the perfect goodness of
an all-powerful and all-knowing God but also the perfect goodness of
such a being requires hell. Hence, the problem of hell is resolved.

One issue remains, however, for in the Introduction I pointed
out that an adequate solution to the problem of hell is subject to
both philosophical and theological constraints. To this point, little
attention has been paid to theological constraints, and before ending

this discussion some is necessary. One such constraint is of singular importance, for the major religions that give rise to the problem of hell each have their own sacred texts that constrain in some fashion or other what an acceptable account of hell can include and exclude. In the concluding chapter, I take a more global perspective on the problem of hell, but to this point I have been focusing on the problem of hell within Christianity. Hence, the relevant theological constraint to be considered is whether the composite view of hell violates appropriate biblical constraints on an adequate view of hell. Does the philosophical account mesh well with the language of scripture, or does this account present yet another example of the conflict between reason and the faith of historical Christianity? I argue that the composite view is consonant both with the language of scripture and with the overall thrust of the eschatological dimension of Christianity as presented in the Bible.

The account of hell presented so far is true to the biblical record in that hell, like heaven, issues from a stable divine character, the primary constituent of which is love. I have insisted on this conception of the divine character in our understanding of hell. The most radical expression of this love occurs in annihilation. In loving a person, one must be willing to suffer even total loss in allowing another to pursue what they most deeply want. This result is of singular importance to this project and in particular to the issue of the relationship between the philosophical account of hell and appropriate theological constraints on an account of hell, for this picture of the undying love of God for humanity is just what a sensitive reading of the sacred literature of the Christian religion reveals.

Yet, apart from the overall biblical picture of God's character, what of the biblical language of hell? Perhaps it can be granted that the account of hell presented here is faithful to the biblical portrait of a loving God. Nevertheless, there is still the language of hell, the weeping and gnashing of teeth, the fire that is not quenched, and the worm that dieth not. What are we to say about these? Worse yet, it might appear that the account presented here is incompatible with this language or, at the very least, can find no place for it. These appearances are misleading, and we can complete a defense of the claim that the composite view of hell satisfies the theological constraint under consideration by looking at what the biblical language of hell says about the experience of those who reject God.

One of the passages most frequently referred to in giving a summary of the biblical portrait of hell is Jesus' parable of the rich man and Lazarus. In fact, one can almost read off the strong view of hell from Jesus' telling of the story. The retributive aspect can be elicited from Abraham's remonstrance to the rich man to remember that "in his lifetime he received his good things." The No Escape Thesis is found in the claim of a "great gulf fixed" between the rich man and Lazarus so that no passage between the two locations is possible. Furthermore, the Existence Thesis and Anti-Universalism Thesis are contained in the story by virtue of the conscious existence of the rich man in a place of torment.

We should nonetheless be suspicious of reading doctrinal statements into Jesus' parable here.[8] We have good reason to treat this story as a parable, and good reason to resist the inclination to elicit doctrinal positions from parables. Instead, the author of a parable constructs a story to make a point, and we should pay heed to the point and not the details of the story. Moreover, the point of this story has nothing to do with the afterlife. Instead, it is a story about the five brothers and the fact that "even if one were to rise from the dead, they would not believe."[9] Why Jesus might have chosen such a story to convey this point is unclear, but it is surely inappropriate to limit the creative power of the storyteller to stories that are true to the facts in every detail.

Putting the parable aside, then, let us consider the remainder of scriptural teaching about hell. The biblical record portrays hell as the end for those who reject God, residence in which is the result of a sentence imposed at the final judgment, a sentence that accords no second chance at reconciliation. Consignment to hell[10] is pictured in terms of punishment, with vivid imagery of its residents in flames, caught up in weeping and gnashing of teeth, "where their worm does not die, and the fire is not quenched," coresidents with Satan and his minions who are "tormented day and night for ever and ever." Although the biblical record does not straightforwardly imply that the exile doctrine is correct (as opposed to the annihilation doctrine), the metaphors and symbols employed in scripture are highly suggestive of this view.

How does this language fit in with the account of hell presented here? First, a sensitive interpretation of the biblical record must juxtapose the metaphor of fire and flames to the metaphor of outer darkness that is also used to describe hell. One need not attempt to imagine one thing of which both descriptions are literally true. They are metaphors in that, applied literally, they generate an inconsistency (because flames produce light).[11] What they signal is something that is objectively as bad as anything can be, and one need not impugn the goodness of God by making him out to be a master torturer in order for hell to be as bad as anything can be. The composite account of hell presented here, in which the end state of hell is nonexistence, is quite naturally viewed as just such an account, an account in which hell is as bad as anything can be (compatible with God's perfect goodness).

We might also interpret the language of fire and flames as signaling an important sense in which God is active in the lives of those in hell because they do not want heaven; it may be, that is, that God continues to intervene in the lives of those who reject him, and the purpose of this intervention may be still that they come to choose the company of heaven. Such intervention would still count as love, but the experience of such love might be painful indeed. Not much understanding of life is needed to know that the commitment of those who desire the highest and best for us has not always led to our comfort. What would be incompatible with the composite account of hell would be to interpret the language of fire and flames in terms of torture or gratuitous suffering of any sort, but there is no exegetical reason to be found for such a view anyway.

Scripture also speaks of hell as a place of punishment, and yet the account of hell presented here does not affirm the Retributive Thesis or involve a retributive punishment model of hell. Instead, it involves a self-determination model of hell, in that those who are in hell are there precisely because it is the only alternative compatible with what they have chosen. Yet failure to embrace a punishment model of hell does not imply that hell is not a place of punishment. In fact, the account of hell presented here clearly does involve punishment in one very obvious sense. One ends up in hell because of one's developed nature, and hell involves being deprived of the most significant good there is. To say that the theory of hell presented here does not involve a retributive punishment model of hell is only to say that God's primary motivation in sending people to hell is not to punish them. His primary motivation is always love, and in loving the depraved he is forced to act in such a way that persons in hell are punished. To think that hell, on the composite view, does not involve punishment is to adopt an incorrect posture on the nature of punishment: That punishment occurs only when motivated by retribution and for the cause of retribution. On such a view of punishment, our penal system would rarely count as a system of punishment, and that implication is sufficient for rejecting the view of punishment according to which the composite view of hell involves no punishment. All that can be said correctly of the composite view is that, on it, God's primary aim in consigning people to hell is not to punish them. However, such a claim takes us beyond the claims of scripture that hell is a place of punishment, so the absence of such a motive on the composite view of hell in no way makes it liable to violating any theological constraints imposed by the biblical record.

The last remaining issue concerns the biblical emphasis on a final judgment and the lack of a second chance at reconciliation with God. The role of a final judgment is already built into the account of hell presented here. At some point after death a determination must be made as to whether one will go to heaven or hell. Whether one should think of this point as occurring immediately after death or at some future time is a theological matter to be decided on grounds other than those directly involved in the account of hell, and so I bypass that issue here. The question the present account of hell must face, however, is whether it is compatible with the *finality* of the final judgment. For instance, is it compatible with the fact that there is no second chance at reconciliation in the biblical record?

One can interpret the notion of a second chance in such a way that any theory that fails to include the No Escape Thesis is committed to a doctrine of a second chance. However, this interpretation should not be accepted. Instead, to have a second chance is to have certain consequences of one's choices deferred while one tries again to avoid those consequences. The account of hell presented here does not imply the existence of this kind of second chance.

Still, what of the emphasis on the finality of the final judgment? The best way to approach this issue is to consider what it aims at denying. The point of the emphasis on the finality in scripture is that, at some point in time, it is too late. Time has run out so that one's options have been delimited to a single option. The finality results when the only option available to one is that of hell; in some sense, the choice of heaven is no longer open to one.

The normal way to understand this restricting of options is in terms of some special activity on the part of God. It is usually thought that at some point God eliminates the possibility of heaven for some individuals. Nothing in the account of finality here, however, requires this construal. A different possibility—one affirmed by the accounts of hell presented by Swinburne and Lewis, which we discussed here and in the previous chapter, as well as the composite view defended here—is that heaven becomes closed to one by virtue of one's own choices and decisions. Furthermore, scripture itself seems to suggest such a position. Consider Jesus' discussion of the sin of blaspheming against the Holy Spirit in Matthew 12. The context involves a charge by the Pharisees, "It is only by Beelzebub, the prince of demons, that this fellow drives out demons" (v. 23). In the course of responding to this charge, Jesus says, "And so I tell you, every sin and blasphemy will be forgiven men, but the blasphemy against the Spirit will not be forgiven" (v. 31). Why would such a sin not be forgiven, and what relevance does this remark by Jesus have to the context in which he is accused of performing miracles by the power of Beelzebub? I want to suggest that a good interpretation of Jesus' remark results when we attribute to him the view that the sin cannot be forgiven because there is nothing left for God to do to secure repentance in some people. The context of this saying is one in which the Pharisees attribute Jesus' power to the prince of demons. Assuming that the quote is actually something Jesus said, Jesus' remarks may have resulted in part from his view that God has come among these people and displayed his power through Jesus himself, and they have interpreted it as demonic; that is, Jesus may have been thinking that God has done all he could do to show himself to these people. He has condescended to live among them and minister to them, and they have chosen to see his work as that of the devil. What remains for God to do to secure fellowship with them? Perhaps Jesus is saying that nothing more could be done, and so forgiveness is no longer possible.

Regardless of the interpretive merits of this suggestion, it does provide an alternative account of the finality of the final judgment. At some point, the infinite love of God has been displayed in the most persuasive way to motivate the pursuit of union with God. Persons have encountered the embodiment of complete goodness, they have been exposed to incomparable beauty, and yet they refuse to see things as they really are; they choose to view God and his love as repulsive. They choose, perhaps, to take the same attitude toward what is truly sublime as is appropriately taken only toward the demonic. What is left for God to do? He has done all he can, and it has been rejected by an unfathomable darkness of mind and soul. The situation is, in a word, hopeless.

This interpretation of the finality of the final judgment has a theoretical cost when combined with the view that it is at the end of one's earthly life that the situation becomes hopeless in this way. This latter view appears strongly in the message of Jesus, for the Gospels consistently portray him as holding that one's present earthly life is of ultimate significance. To explain the finality of the final judgment, given that this finality is achieved at the end of one's present earthly life, an additional assumption is needed to the effect that a complete encounter with God has occurred at some point in each person's earthly life. This assumption may seem questionable to some, but there is no philosophical or theological reason to deny it. Assumptions could be made about what a complete encounter with God must be like that would make such an encounter unlikely on empirical grounds to occur for every person.[12] An investigation of these matters takes us well beyond the scope of this work, however, so I confine my remarks to a suggestion. I suggest that any version of Christianity that holds that one's afterlife state is determined solely by one's present earthly life and also holds that some but not all have had a complete encounter with God in this present earthly life is morally problematic. On such a view, the fairness of God is impugned, just as the fairness of parents is impugned when they give gifts to only some of their children. Given this fact, there seems to be no reason whatsoever for thinking inadequate the account of the finality of the final judgment that is compatible with the composite account of hell presented here.

So even though the strictly philosophical investigation of the doctrine of hell does not imply many of the aspects of biblical teaching about hell, including that one's earthly life is of ultimate significance, that is not a telling criticism of this study. Nothing in the composite view of hell is incompatible with any appropriate theological constraint on an account of hell arising from the authority of the Christian scriptures.

Conclusion

The results we have achieved concerning a proper account of hell can be summarized as follows. A Self-Determination Thesis replaces the Retribution Thesis. Those in hell are there because of their determination to avoid the company of the redeemed and the God who redeems. As F. F. Bruce says regarding the gulf between the rich man and Lazarus, "the impassable gulf, in fact, was of the rich man's own creating."[13] The No Escape Thesis is also to be rejected, although the account is compatible with the view that there is no hope of escaping hell. The difference between this claim and the No Escape Thesis is that the latter states that there is nothing one can do, change, or become to get out of hell once one is consigned there, whereas the interpretation of the former claim can focus attention on what could be done to secure a favorable opinion in the heart of a person regarding presence in heaven. Of course, God could always bludgeon one into submission, but presence in heaven requires something more delicate, for the goal is a person governed by a love of God and a delight in his beauty. Furthermore, neither the Anti-Universalism Thesis nor the Existence Thesis is to be accepted. Both theses may be true and they may not, but neither is necessarily true. If it is possible to be characterized by a determination to avoid heaven, it is equally possible that no one is to be so characterized. So the doctrine of hell itself holds no promise that some persons will exist in hell. In addition, although it is possible for persons to have hell as a place of residence or state of existence, it is also possible that those consigned to hell undergo a complete and total eradication of being.

Notes

1. I choose this term with some misgivings, for the annihilation doctrine of hell must not be confused with the annihilation view of hell discussed in chapter 2 which accepts all of (H1)–(H4) except (H2), the Existence Thesis. The annihilation doctrine is, at this point, committed only to denying (H2).

2. The qualifier 'if we can trust their word' is meant to be taken seriously. Although the freedom they take to be correlated with the nonexistence of God is overwhelming, how the existence of God could give rise to a structure of meaningfulness not equally problematic is not clear. The freedom they think arises from the nonexistence of God occurs because they can imagine only anything other than a creator God giving objective ontological grounding to values. If there is no God, there is only whatever value persons can create for themselves, thus resulting in the question of whether one's own life is truly meaningful. The question of the meaningfulness of life here is, I think, misplaced; I can see no reason to think that there being a God who created us by itself solves some deep dilemma about the meaningfulness of life (although, of course, this should not be taken to mean that I think life with God is meaningless). If life could have no meaning apart from God, it is not clear how anything external to oneself could suddenly infuse one's life with meaning, for what has meaning in this sense is what one is "attached to." Christians (myself included) believe that the deepest fulfillment one can have comes in properly relating oneself to God, but that is a different issue from the issue of the meaningfulness of life. If life is not meaningful *from the inside*, nothing can give it meaning. Even if the existence of God is granted and his existence implies that certain things are objectively valuable that would not be otherwise, that in no way solves the question of whether a person is attached to, or attracted to, what is valuable.

Perhaps, however, existentialists are completely "attached to" God, so that with him all would be well (whatever is objectively valuable because of him they treasure) and without him nothing matters. (In this respect, devoted Christians and atheistic existentialists are more alike than are devoted Christians and those who take the name of Christianity for social or other mundane purposes; for devoted Christians are as much "attached to" God as are the existentialists [they only disagree about the facts], whereas those who take the name of Christianity for mundane purposes are usually attached ultimately to something other than God.) If existentialists are completely attached to God in this way, however, the features that give rise to the issue of suicide are internal to the person rather than external, concerning the existence of God. If the issue is to be an external, objective one, existentialists could claim at best that if God existed and they obtained eternal bliss with him eternally, they may no longer think or care about the question of the meaningfulness of life, but, strictly speaking, God's existence and their relationship with him does not give meaning to their lives unless they find satisfied in him the deepest longings of their soul—and that is a subjective matter, not an objective one.

3. A theory of rational belief elucidating and clarifying many of the complexities involved in this rough formulation can be found in Richard Foley, *The Theory of Epistemic Rationality* (Cambridge, Mass., 1987). Foley used to call this sense of rationality the *epistemic* sense, but he has more recently come to label it the *egocentric* sense. See, for example, his "Reply to Alston, Feldman and Swain," *Philosophy and Phenomenological Research* 50 (September 1989): 169–188; and *Working Without a Net: Essays in Egocentric Epistemology* (New York, 1993).

4. For a defense of this doctrine, see my *The Possibility of an All-Knowing God* (London, 1986).

5. For arguments against the existence of such counterfactuals regarding what free individuals would do, see Robert M. Adams, "Middle Knowledge and the Problem of Evil," *American Philosophical Quarterly* 14 (1977): 109–117.

6. The most recent defense of this view is by William Hasker in *God, Time, and Knowledge* (Ithaca, N.Y., 1989).

7. I have defended the compatibility thesis in *The Possibility of an All-Knowing God*, chapters 4 and 5.

8. See George Eldon Ladd, *A Theology of the New Testament* (Grand Rapids, 1975), p. 194.

9. Ibid.

10. I am, for the moment, ignoring the distinction between *hades* and *gehenna*, aiming more at providing a summary of the popular understanding of the biblical record than one that is exegetically careful.

11. The inconsistency here is not a logical inconsistency, but rather an inconsistency with the laws of nature. That distinction, however, seems irrelevant here. The remarks about fire and brimstone and the like are supposed to have a point to them, and it is hard to see how any point could be made by telling us supposedly literally true things which we cannot imagine or picture being literally true. The point, it would seem, must be something beyond the literal meaning of the descriptions.

12. For example, some might use Peter's remark in Acts 4:12 before the

Sanhedrin ("Salvation is found in no one else; for there is no other name under heaven given to men by which we must be saved," *New International Version*) to infer that the biblical view is that in order to be saved one must know of the historical person Jesus. Many questions have to be answered before this view is accepted, but we can get to the heart of the issue by noting that the passage can equally well be interpreted otherwise. For example, it can equally mean only that no one is saved except through the work of Jesus, and that claim can be true regardless of whether one lived with Jesus, as Peter did, long before the birth of Jesus, as did Abraham, or long after Jesus in places Christianity never reached.

The worry conservative Christians will have about this interpretive maneuver is that it allows for faith in Jesus to occur even though one is unaware of who Jesus is. I do not have the space to address this issue fully here, but a suggestive remark might be helpful. What is important to conservative Christianity about the work of Jesus regarding eternal salvation involves his deity. For conservative Christians it is the fact that Jesus is God that makes salvation possible by reliance on what he has done for one. It is because one is depending on God himself to undertake to resolve the human condition that faith in Jesus is effective for salvation. Given the space, I would argue that conservative Christians should think of this dependence on God himself as crucial for salvation. It allows a unified account of salvation for both Old and New Testaments, whereas the alternative required some disjoint account that holds forth different requirements for salvation depending on whether one lived before or after Jesus.

13. F. F. Bruce, *The Hard Saying of Jesus* (Downers Grove, Ill., 1983), pp. 187–188.

5

A Global Perspective on the Problem of Hell

To this point this book has approached the problem of hell from the provincial perspective of Christianity. As pointed out in the Introduction, I followed this procedure to take advantage of the history of dialogue on the problem within that tradition, whereas a procedure that attempted to address the problem from a more global perspective would have had no such history on which to draw. It is time, however, to step back from the particular claims of Christianity to take a broader view of the problem of hell, to see what general religious commitments give rise to the problem and what possible solutions are available to a religious perspective once the problem arises.

Our investigation has shown that the religious commitments that generate the problem of hell are quite minimal. The problem of hell arises once one affirms a traditional conception of God—omnipotent, omniscient, perfectly good, and the creator of the universe—together with a religious outlook that has an eschatological component with afterlife significance. The problem of hell is thus independent of the differences between various religious outlooks on issues such as the possibility of reincarnation, the mechanism of salvation or enlightenment, the truth of monotheism, and a variety of other religious controversies. The problem of hell arises at a level of religious commitment more basic than many of these controversial issues and, as such, is a problem best thought of as independent of any particular religion.

Moreover, the commitments that generate the problem of hell also circumscribe the possible avenues to explore in attempting to solve the problem. Unlike the more general problem of evil, the problem of hell is unlikely to be solved by giving up on the doctrines of omnipotence or omniscience. In any religious outlook, it will not have escaped God's notice that his goal for humankind requires a contrast, which is hell. To improvise on one's concept of God to such an extent is to debase God, for even finite humans understand the way in which hell is related to God's ultimate purposes. Protesting that God is not as mighty as some have thought and hence cannot do anything about hell will not do, for in any of the religious outlooks that give rise to the problem of hell, the fundamental afterlife options are present as the result of God's direct activity. So, God could have at least avoided making either alternative. Instead, any solution to the problem of hell will have to deal with the nature of God's goodness and the motivations he has for creating the possibilities of heaven and hell in the first place.

So the question arises as to what possible motivations God could have for creating the possibilities of heaven and hell. Here the logical possibilities abound, but the religiously tolerable range of possibilities is quite small. Viewed solely from the perspective of logical possibility, God might create heaven and hell for the sheer fun of it, to give himself something to do, or for any of a number of other reasons that would have little suasive power for those who view human life as having eternal significance. The religious possibilities seem more limited, limited to those motives having to do in some way or other with God's goodness. The possibility of heaven, if it is to have religious significance, would seem to be connected directly to God's care and concern for what he has created, that is to say, to his goodness. What about God's goodness could function as a motive in creating heaven and hell? The goodness of an individual is constituted by a number of different character traits, some of which are motivational and some of which are not, but the goodness of an individual itself is not a motivating characteristic, except indirectly. A person's honesty can prompt truth telling, and so the goodness of that individual—of which being honest is partly constitutive—can indirectly prompt action. So, the question we need to ask is what character traits go into God's goodness that might motivate the afterlife alternatives of heaven and hell? Discussion of this question has produced two answers—love and justice—and any other religiously adequate answers are difficult to imagine.

A global perspective on the problem of hell quickly arrives, then, at the position where an adequate conception of hell must be grounded in either God's love or his justice. This divide separates the strong view of hell and simple alternatives to it from the issuant conceptions discussed in the previous two chapters. As we have seen, the hard core of the strong view and its simple alternatives is the retributive punishment model of hell, a model according to which hell is firmly grounded in the justice of God. In contrast, the issuant conceptions offered by Lewis and Stump and the composite view of hell defended here locate the doctrine of hell in God's love.

Before reaching the conclusion that the alternatives examined in this work are the right ones to consider not only from the provincial standpoint of Christianity but also from a more global standpoint, we need to consider whether there is any way of explaining hell as based on God's justice without affirming the retributive punishment model of hell. In particular, we must consider nonretributive conceptions of justice, those that emphasize reform and deterrence. It is difficult to see how to get much mileage out of the idea that consignment to hell is justified by its deterrent effect. The warnings one gets about hell in one's earthly life might be claimed to have some such effect, and perhaps the punishment of those in hell might be claimed as well to have a deterrent effect on those in heaven by preventing them from wanting to escape. The problem with either attempt to justify hell in terms of deterrence is that it must be combined with a retributive aspect in order to avoid unjustly sending some to hell for the purpose of deterrence. Without a retributive aspect, sending some of the redeemed to hell would succeed as well, perhaps those thought wrongly by humans to deserve hell. So a deterrence account of justice appears unlikely to offer an acceptable account of hell, for the same reasons that a deterrence theory of punishment is problematic.

One way to try to salvage a deterrence account of hell from this objection deserves mention. One could hold that God consigns to hell on the basis of some decree that one goes to hell if and only if one's past was characterized by certain conditions, where the justification for the decree was deterrent in character. This approach cannot salvage a deterrence basis for hell from my previous objection, for the basis for consignment to hell in this new deterrence approach is still retributive: It concerns whether one's past is characterized by certain conditions. Once this feature is noted, the question immediately arises whether the consignment is fair, that is, whether the punishment is justified by the character of the offense. An answer to this question in terms of the deterrence such a practice achieves fails to address the concern, for it is easy to construct counterexamples in which deterrence is achieved by drastically unfair punishments. So the only recourse such a deterrence approach could have is to argue that the punishment was fair in terms of the relationship between crime and punishment, and that recourse burdens the deterrence approach with all of the problems of the retributive model of hell. So the prospects for basing hell on a deterrent conception of justice seem dim.

Reform presents a better alternative than deterrence, one that is also distinct from an account that centers on retribution. On this approach, those in hell are there until they have been reformed to the extent that they are fit for heaven. Such a view obscures the distinction between justice-based and love-based accounts of hell, for this alternative might just as easily be described as grounded in God's love as well as in his justice. As any good parent knows, sometimes the only good way to love children is to discipline them.

Nonetheless, such a theory of hell has a distinct disadvantage. Although such a theory is compatible with a religious outlook claiming significance for one's present earthly life beyond the grave, it is in tension with a truly eschatological significance for life. The idea of hell based on the possibility of reform turns hell into something like a halfway house on the way to heaven. No such halfway house is truly hell, for hell, as understood in this book, is the ultimate contrast to heaven and not a possible route to it. Such a view does not solve the problem of hell by giving an acceptable account of hell. Rather, it addresses the problem of hell by abandoning the notion altogether.

There is one way to try to develop the idea of hell as based on God's reforming justice without abandoning the notion of hell altogether. One might hold that the point of the halfway house to heaven was to reform and make fit for heaven, but also allow that the task might fail. In such a case, the halfway house would be, for some, a permanent dwelling rather than a temporary one. Such a view cannot, however, explain permanent residence in hell in terms of God's motive to reform one. The most natural response to give in order to explain such permanent residence appeals to the resistance of the resident to reform. In such a case, the view no longer explains permanent residence in terms of God's reforming justice, but rather in terms of the character and choices of the individual in hell. The important point to note about this change in the account is that it is most amenable to the issuant conceptions of hell discussed in the last two chapters, and in particular to those issuant conceptions that substitute a Self-Determination Thesis to explain permanent residence in hell for an explanation centering on God's justice, however conceived. Thus, the conclusion to which we are led is that if hell is based on God's desire to reform the inhabitants of hell, the doctrine of hell should be abandoned altogether, even if the view that there is life after the grave is retained.

It may be, however, that a religious perspective should abandon eschatological elements altogether and interpret the language of heaven and hell as indicators of the possibility of future life being better or worse than present earthly life. In such a view, no permanence would be attached either to being in "heaven" or to being in "hell."[1] As such, the view would posit something very much akin to endless reincarnation, although without any claim that life beyond the grave involved another earthly life with another earthly death. Although a possibility, such a view is psychologically unsatisfying, as is shown by the fact that religions that posit the possibility of an endless cycle of rebirths also posit a possibility of escape from this cycle. This remark, however, is not an argument against non-eschatological accounts of the afterlife. Instead, the locus in which the problem of hell arises is assumed from the outset to involve eschatological significance to life beyond the grave.

Once conceptions of justice involving reform and deterrence are abandoned and a retributive conception of justice is affirmed, however, one encounters the problems with resting an account of hell on a retributive punishment model. As our investigation of the doctrine of hell in Christianity showed, the prospects for a successful resolution of the problem of hell on such a model are dim indeed. What is left, then, is to base hell on God's love as opposed to his justice. Once such an approach is taken, I submit that the solution to the problem of hell is to be found in the composite view of hell defended in the last chapter. I will not repeat the arguments that lead to that view here, but keep in mind that the discussion of issuant conceptions of hell proceeds from a general characterization of the nature of God neutral between competing theistic religions. As such, the course of the dialectic that leads to the conclusion that the composite view is correct is as suited for the global context of religious neutrality as it was for the provincial context of Christianity. Such a view grounds hell in God's love, and it need not sacrifice the eschatological significance of hell, for it can include a claim to the effect that there is no hope of leaving hell, although this account of the eschatological significance of hell is quite different from the No Escape Thesis required by a retributive punishment model of hell. On the composite view, hell is the ultimate and only contrast to heaven by virtue of the fact that its teleological character is annihilation. It does not imply that everyone, or even anyone, is annihilated, but that fact does not affect the significance of the point that the goal of hell is annihilation, for this goal undergirds the eschatological character of hell.

So the only remaining alternative to the composite account defended here is one that claims there is ultimately no contrast to heaven; there are only different routes to it. Such a view is, however, a version of necessary universalism that is subject to the difficulties for that view described in chapter 2. The proper conclusion to draw, then, is that the problem of hell as it develops within Christianity is but a microcosm of how the problem can be addressed more globally.

In the context of Christianity, discussion naturally begins with the strong view of hell, which affirms that hell is a place of retributive punishment for those whose earthly lives warrant it, where some people will exist eternally, incapable of escape even with the help of an omnipotent creator. I argued in chapter 1 that this view is subject to moral, epistemological, and conceptual difficulties. Because the strong view is composed of four separate theses, the inadequacy of the strong view might be remedied by dropping one of the four commitments. The views that result from such elimination include the typical alternatives to the strong view found in the history of the doctrine of hell in Christianity—annihilationism, universalism, and second chance theories—and in chapter 2, we found that these views make little if any progress in solving the problem of hell. So in chapters 3 and 4, a more fundamental inquiry was undertaken toward finding a solution to the problem of hell by explicitly accounting for hell in terms of the nature of God. Such a procedure results in what I have called an issuant conception of hell, the investigation of which was completed with a formulation and defense of a composite view of hell. On the composite view, hell is viewed as a system having a functional or teleological component, which is annihilation, implemented in a certain way or displayed in a certain mechanism. The need for the second component derives from the fact that annihilation is, we might say, the limit of hell and not necessarily its substance, or, put differently, hell is a journey beyond death toward annihilation, but with the possibility that the journey is never completed. I have had little to say about the mechanism of hell, the way such a journey should be thought to occur if one holds a theistic view that requires a doctrine of hell, but my intent was not to speculate about the details of hell but rather to address the problem of hell. In the composite view, I argued, a solution to that problem is found.

If we think of the doctrine of hell in terms of the ordinary conception and the common alternatives to it, the doctrine of hell defended here has much greater affinity to the strong view of hell than to such alternatives as universalism, second chance views, and perhaps even annihilationism or conditional immortality. Like the strong view, the composite view denies that there is any comfort in supposing that all may, in the end, partake of the heavenly community. Furthermore, this view does not imply the existence of a second chance for redemption after death and hence is compatible with the biblical language about the finality of death. The only way the present view is weaker on this point than the strong view is that the present view denies that the impossibility of escape from hell is due to anything outside the control of the individual resident of hell. The strong view makes leaving hell impossible because God will not and could not let it happen; the composite view explains any impossibility of escape from the prison of hell in terms of locks on the inside rather than on the outside. Perhaps most surprisingly, the present view is at least as near the strong view as it is to annihilationism. I say "surprisingly," for the defended account maintains that the teleological nature of hell is nothingness. Nonetheless, this account is not a version of annihilationism or conditional immortalism. According to annihilationism, eternal life is only a gift for the elect, and all who reject God of necessity cease to be. The view of hell offered here is compatible with both the annihilationist implication that no one exists in hell and with the implication of the strong view that all persons exist eternally. Whether it is closer to annihilationism than to the strong view is difficult to determine because one would have to know what the psychology of persons will be like in the afterlife. If persons are capable of employing self-deception and other defense mechanisms eternally, perhaps no one will ever achieve the rationality of thought and will necessary on the proffered account of hell to warrant annihilation. If so, then the present account is much closer to the strong view than to annihilationism. Having much confidence in judgments about psychology in the afterlife is difficult, however. In light of this fact, I make no judgment of comparison as to the closeness of the present view to the strong view versus annihilationism.

The fundamental virtue of the view of hell presented here over the strong view is that this view issues out of God's love. The difficulties facing the strong view of hell can be traced to the fact that it does not so issue from God; in a word, it is not an issuant conception of hell at all. Because of this fact, it is irremediably objectionable on both moral and epistemological grounds. In this way, the view of hell presented here is more like the heretical alternatives than it is like the strong view, for the heretical alternatives typically place a much greater emphasis on the love of God in describing hell than does the strong view. In summary, the issuant conception of hell defended here is much closer *in its substance* to the strong view than to common alternatives, but it is not as close *in its defense*.

In this last respect, annihilationism (the view that denies only the Existence Thesis among those theses affirmed by the strong view) is no better off than the strong view. It is no more an issuant conception of hell than is the strong view. Because of this fact, it has no more resources for addressing the problem of hell than does the strong view.

Both universalism and second chance views may count as issuant conceptions of hell, for they include a strong emphasis on the loving nature of God in characterizing the options for humanity in the afterlife. Neither theory is very plausible, however. Necessary universalism founders on the rock of human freedom, for it is not a necessary truth that God can always do something to secure a loving response from a free individual. Contingent universalism is a nonstarter on the problem of hell, for it only modally masks the problem of hell. It focuses on maintaining the actual goodness of God, but at the expense of his perfect and essential goodness. Second chance doctrines are even more problematic, for what problem a second chance is supposed to solve is not clear. If it is necessary for securing the justice of hell that persons not be judged on the basis of their past actions alone but that they be given another chance to avoid hell, additional chances will be necessary as well, if the second chance is not taken. Second chance doctrines then quickly become infinite chance doctrines, and infinitely delayed consequences for sin are no consequences at all. Alternatively, if a second chance is not necessary for securing the justice of hell, why anyone would proffer such an account as an alternative to the strong view of hell is not clear. Either way, then, second chance doctrines fail to make any progress past the strong view in solving the problem of hell.

The conception of hell defended here distinguishes the formal features of hell from its substantive reality. The teleological nature of hell is nonbeing; in the end, there is no force, place, or way of being that is the antithesis of the being and nature of God. The substantive reality of hell, however, is determined not only by a clear understanding of the logical alternative to the presence and blessings of God but also by the condition of those who do not choose the company of heaven. In particular, persons can fail to be fit for either heaven or annihilation in two ways, one cognitive and one affective. Persons can organize their picture of the world and their responses to the lessons experience tries to teach by refusing to countenance either the existence of God or the possibility of heaven. In the face of such recalcitrance, perhaps God can do nothing, compatible with honoring the free decisions his creatures make, to correct this faulty conceptual scheme. Furthermore, persons can have conflicting desires. They can wish for heaven without being willing to take the steps necessary for securing it. In addition, many individuals choose irrationally and on the spur of the moment; many choose that which, on a moment's reflection, they would realize they do not want. The doctrine of hell needs to be structured to take account of these possibilities, and thus the present account posits a substantial reality of hell involving actual existence for those whose choices do not meet the requisite characteristics for annihilation. The intent of God in forming the mechanism of hell is for people to come to see the options clearly enough that they see the overwhelming desirability of eternal life over eternal death; because that may not be possible without violating their freedom, the secondary goal of ridding them of irrationality and instability in their conception of and desire for things is pursued. If the mechanism accomplishes this goal, annihilation results; if not, the process can go on eternally.

Note

1. I put the terms 'heaven' and 'hell' in quotes to signify that the usage of these terms here deviates from the interpretation I have given them for the purposes of this book. To reiterate, I use these terms only in the context of religious views that posit eschatological significance for life beyond the grave.

Bibliography

Adams, Marilyn. "Divine Justice, Divine Love, and the Life to Come." *Crux* 13 (1976–1977), pp. 12–28.

——. "Hell and the God of Justice," *Religious Studies* 11 (1975), pp. 433–447.

Adams, Robert M. "Middle Knowledge and the Problem of Evil." *American Philosophical Quarterly* 14 (1977), pp. 109–117.

Ahern, M. B. *The Problem of Evil.* London, 1971.

Alston, William P. "The Inductive Argument From Evil and the Human Cognitive Condition." In *Philosophical Perspectives 5: Philosophy of Religion,* James E. Tomberlin, editor. Atascadero, Calif., 1991.

Barth, Karl. *Church Dogmatics,* G. W. Bromiley and T. F. Torrance, editors. Edinburgh, 1936–1969.

Bruce, F. F. *The Hard Saying of Jesus.* Downers Grove, Ill., 1983.

Brunner, Emil. *Eternal Hope,* Harold Knight, translator. Philadelphia, 1954.

Buswell, Oliver. *A Systematic Theology of the Christian Religion.* Grand Rapids, 1962.

Chesen, E. S. *Religion May Be Hazardous to Your Health.* New York, 1972.

Cullman, Oscar. *Immortality of the Soul or Resurrection of the Dead?* New York, 1964.

Edwards, Jonathan. *The Nature of True Virtue.* Ann Arbor, 1960, originally published in *Two Dissertations* (Boston, 1788).

Fitzpatrick, F. J. "The Onus of Proof in Arguments About the Problem of Evil." *Religious Studies* 17 (1981): 63–79.

Flint, Thomas P., editor. *Christian Philosophy.* Notre Dame, 1990.

Foley, Richard. "Reply to Alston, Feldman and Swain." *Philosophy and Phenomenological Research* 50.1 (September 1989), pp. 169–188.

——. *The Theory of Epistemic Ratinality.* Cambridge, 1986.

——. *Working Without a Net: Essays in Egocentric Epistemology.* New York, 1992.

Geach, Peter. *Providence and Evil.* Cambridge, 1977.

Hasker, William. *God, Time, and Knowledge.* Ithaca, N.Y., 1989.

Hebblethwaite, Brian. *The Christian Hope.* Basingstoke, 1984.

Helm, Paul, editor. *Divine Commands and Morality.* Oxford, 1981.

Irwin, Terence. *Plato's Moral Theory.* Oxford, 1977.

Jurieu, Pierre. *Apologie pour les Réformateurs.* Rotterdam, 1683.

Küng, Hans. *Eternal Life?* Edward Quinn, translator. Garden City, N.Y., 1984.

Kvanvig, Jonathan L. *The Possibility of an All-Knowing God.* London, 1986.

——, and McCann, Hugh J. "Divine Conservation and the Persistence of the World." In *Divine and Human Action: Essays in the Metaphysics of Theism,* Thomas V. Morris, editor. Ithaca, N.Y., 1988.

Ladd, George Eldon. *A Theology of the New Testament.* Grand Rapids, 1975.

Lakatos, Imre. "Falsification and the Methodology of Scientific Research Programmes." In *Criticism and the Growth of Knowledge,* Imre Lakatos and Alan Musgrave, editors. Cambridge, 1970.

Leibniz, Gottfried Wilhelm. *Essais de théodicée sur la bonté de Dieu, la liberté de l'homme, et origene du mal.* Amsterdam, 1734.

Lewis, C. S. *The Problem of Pain.* London, 1948.

Lewis, David. *Counterfactuals.* Oxford, 1973.

Macquarrie, John. *Principles of Christian Theology.* New York, 1966.

Malebranche, Nicolas. *Dialogues on Metaphysics and on Religion,* Morris Ginsberg, translator. London, 1923.

McCann, Hugh J., and Kvanvig, Jonathan L. "The Occasionalist Proselytizer: A Modified Catechism." In *Philosophical Perspectives 5: Philosophy of Religion,* James E. Tomberlin, editor. Atascadero, Calif., 1991.

McTaggart, John. *Some Dogmas of Religion.* London, 1906.

Morris, Thomas V. *Anselmian Explorations.* Notre Dame, 1987.

Morris, Thomas V. "Duty and Divine Goodness." *American Philosophical Quarterly* 21 (1984), pp. 261–268.

——. *The Logic of God Incarnate.* Ithaca, N.Y. 1986.

——, editor. *The Concept of God.* New York, 1987.

——. editor. *Divine and Human Action: Essays in the Metaphysics of Theism.* Ithaca, N.Y. 1988.

——, and Menzel, Christopher. "Absolute Creation." *American Philosophical Quarterly* 23 (1986), pp. 353–362.

Pinnock, Clark. "Fire, Then Nothing." *Christianity Today,* March 20, 1987, pp. 40–41.

Plantinga, Alvin. *God, Freedom and Evil.* New York, 1974.

——. *The Nature of Necessity.* Oxford, 1974.

Quinn, Philip. *Divine Commands and Moral Requirements.* Oxford, 1978.

——. "The Recent Revival of Divine Command Ethics." *Philosophy and Phenomenological Research,* vol. 50 supplement (Fall 1990), pp. 345–366.

Reichenbach, Bruce. *Evil and a Good God.* New York, 1982.

Robinson, John A. T. *In the End, God.* New York, 1968.

Stalnaker, Robert. "A Theory of Conditionals." In *Causation and Conditionals*, Ernest Sosa, editor. Oxford, 1975.

Stump, Eleonore. "Dante's Hell, Aquinas's Moral Theory, and the Love of God." *Canadian Journal of Philosophy* 16 (1986), pp. 181–196.

————, and Kretzmann, Norman. "Being and Goodness." In *Divine and Human Action: Essays in the Metaphysics of Theism*, Thomas V. Morris, editor. Ithaca, N.Y., 1988.

Swinburne, Richard. *The Coherence of Theism.* Oxfrod, 1977.

————. "A Theodicy of Heaven and Hell." In *The Existence and Nature of God*, Alfred J. Freddoso, editor. Notre Dame, 1983.

Talbott, Thomas P. "The Doctrine of Everlasting Punishment." *Faith and Philosophy* 7.1 (January 1990), pp. 19–43.

Wainwright, William. "Original Sin." In *Philosophy and the Christian Faith*, Thomas V. Morris, editor. Notre Dame, 1988.

Walker, D. P. *The Decline of Hell.* Chicago, 1964.

Woodward, Kenneth L. "Heaven." *Newsweek*, March 29, 1989, pp. 52–55.

Wykstra, Stephen. "The Humean Obstacle to Evidential Arguments From Suffering: On Avoiding the Evils of 'Appearance'." *International Journal for Philosophy of Religion* 16 (1984), pp. 73–93.

Index

Index